Shakespeare Inside

Shakespeare

Series edited by: Simon Palfrey and Ewan Fernie

Shakespeare Inside
The Bard Behind Bars

Amy Scott-Douglass

continuum

Continuum

The Tower Building
11 York Road
London
SE1 7NX
www.continnumbooks.com

80 Maiden Lane
Suite 704
New York
NY 10038

British Library Cataloguing-in-Publication Data
A catalogue record for this book is available from the British Library.

ISBN-10: HB: 0-8264-8698-3
          PB: 0-8264-8699-1
ISBN-13: HB: 978-0-8264-8698-1
          PB: 978-0-8264-8699-8

Library of Congress Cataloging-in-Publication Data
A catalog record for this book is available from the Library of Congress.

Typeset by BookEns Ltd, Royston, Herts
Printed and bound by Athenaeum Press Ltd, Gateshead, Tyne and Wear.

Contents

Though now we must appear bloody and cruel,
As, by our hands and this our present act,
You see we do, yet see you but our hands
And this the bleeding business they have done.
Our hearts you see not; they are pitiful.

Julius Caesar 3.1.167–71

Acknowledgments

My introduction to prison Shakespeare came in summer of 2003 when I was in Washington DC for the summer, participating in a seminar at the Folger Shakespeare Library and staying with my friend Heather Haines, who at that time worked in the documentary department at the Public Broadcasting Service headquarters. Independent film director Hank Rogerson had sent PBS a video with several scenes from a documentary he was making called *Shakespeare Behind Bars*, and one day Heather came home from work, slapped Hank's video on top of the VCR and proclaimed, 'You have to see this, Amy. You're supposed to see this.' As usual, Heather was right.

When I presented a paper on *Shakespeare Behind Bars* at the Shakespeare and Philosophy conference in Budapest in 2004, the topic and my increasing enthusiasm for it were enough to induce Simon Palfrey and Ewan Fernie to ask me if I would write a short book on prison Shakespeare as part of the *Shakespeare Now!* series. I hadn't wanted to write a whole book, quite frankly. I had only planned to write an article. I had planned, without really realizing it, just to stay in my ivory tower and *read* about the various Shakespeare programs, write up a little piece, throw in some Foucault and Genet and call it a day. To write a book would require actually visiting the prison and meeting the inmates. It would require going beyond theory, or, at least, beyond the theoretical. It would require courage. For a single woman in her early 30s, sitting down to meet with men convicted of crimes against women and girls would require a particular kind of courage. I was scared, to tell you the truth. I was worried what the journey might tell me about myself. Nevertheless, I decided to say yes. Little did I know that going to prison would be the most important and enlightening experience of my adult life.

I am immensely grateful to Simon and Ewan for persuading me to write this book, and to other Shakespeareans and Renaissance scholars who have encouraged my work over the past three years, especially Richard Burt, Courtney Lehmann, Diana Henderson, James Fitzmaurice, Jeremy Lopez, Kenneth Rothwell, and Pete Donaldson. I thank Curt Tofteland for being the first of many prison theatre directors to let me inside his program, and I thank Curt, Marcia Tofteland, Karen Heath, and Michelle Bombe for befriending me once I got there. Most Shakespeare prison directors operate on a voluntary basis; they put their hearts and souls into the work that they do in prison and are about as giving and charitable as people come. When I traveled to visit the prison programs of Jean Trounstine, Agnes Wilcox, Meg Sempreora and Laura Bates, these theatre directors and fellow academics extended the same kind of hospitality towards me, inviting me to stay in their homes and providing me with meals and rides to the airport. I also want to acknowledge the goodwill of Hank Rogerson and Jillan Spitzmiller, who encouraged me to go to Sundance to see the world premiere of their film and supplied me with video and DVD copies in advance of its general release. Most of all, I am indebted to the men and women behind bars for sharing their stories with me. I thank each and every one of them for their intelligence, candor and insight.

In the two and a half years that I spent researching this book, I held tenure-track positions at three different institutions. I am grateful for the financial support some of these institutions provided to help me complete this project, and I am even more grateful for the intellectual and moral support that I received from my colleagues and students. From California State University Fullerton, where I worked from 2000–4, I wish to acknowledge Joanne Gass, Susan Jacobsen, Joe Sawicki, Sherri Sawicki, Kay Stanton, Marlin

Blaine, Dorothea Kehler, Shannon Osborne Ford, Sarah Webster, Janis Okerlund, and Corina Kesler. In 2004, when I moved to New York in order to be closer to my family in Ohio, I found a community of like-minded colleagues in the English department at the State University of New York College at Brockport, including Janie Hinds, Jennifer Haytock, Ralph Black, Steve Fellner, and Sharon Kinsley. At Denison University, which I have been fortunate to call home since 2005, I am so blessed with supportive administrators, encouraging colleagues, and engaged students that my debts are already too numerous to name. My thanks are due to the entire English department faculty, my fellow new faculty initiates (most – if not all – of whom have become my dear, dear friends), my colleagues in Women's Studies and Black Studies, countless students, and the Denison administrators, particularly Provost Keith Boone, who financed the trip my freshmen 'Prison Stages' class took to meet the Shakespeare Behind Bars actors in person.

My deepest thanks are also due to my friends and family, especially Heather Haines, who was responsible for the fateful introduction in the first place; Hilary Trotta Alexander, who helped to relieve my pre-prison anxieties by joking that I should 'strap down' my chest and plan to get her something from the prison gift shop; Donna Woodford, who is unarguably one of the smartest Renaissance scholars on the face of the earth; Adam Kitzes, who offered his invaluable insight at crucial moments; Michael Harris, who was there when it mattered most; and my sister Cyd Schaechterle, who was a constant source of support.

Finally, I never would have been able to write this book were it not for the kindness and generosity of my parents, Gordon and Norma Schaechterle. Years and years from now, I will continue to treasure my memories of the summer I spent with them while writing this manuscript – watching Larry King's televised report from San Quentin with my 76-year-old father and then, later that evening, listening to the strains of Johnny Cash's 'I Walk the Line' and 'Folsom Prison Blues' coming from the old record player in my father's bedroom as he listened to *At San Quentin*, an album I never even knew he had; or looking across a prison stage at my 74-year-old mother, who had driven ten hours, even though she was ill, simply because I asked her to come to the Shakespeare Behind Bars performance of *Comedy of Errors* . . . even (and I will always smile at this), even when she thought that attending the performance 'on the yard' meant we would be sitting on the cold December ground. I am the luckiest person in the world to have such amazing parents. This book is dedicated to them with inexpressible love.

General Editors' Preface

Shakespeare Now! represents a new form for new approaches. Whereas academic writing is far too often ascendant and detached, attesting all too clearly to years of specialist training, *Shakespeare Now!* offers a series of intellectual adventure stories: animate with fresh and often exposed thinking, with ideas still heating in the mind.

This series of 'minigraphs' will thus help to bridge two yawning gaps in current public discourse. First, the gap between scholarly thinking and a public audience: the assumption of academics that they cannot speak to anyone but their peers unless they hopelessly dumb-down their work. Second, the gap between public audience and scholarly thinking: the assumption of regular playgoers, readers, or indeed actors that academics write about the plays at a level of abstraction or specialization that they cannot hope to understand.

But accessibility should not be mistaken for comfort or predictability. Impatience with scholarly obfuscation is usually accompanied by a basic impatience with anything but (supposed) common sense. What this effectively means is a distrust of really thinking, and a disdain for anything that might unsettle conventional assumptions, particularly through crossing or re-drafting formal, political, or theoretical boundaries. We encourage such adventure, and base our claim to a broad audience upon it.

Here, then, is where our series is innovative: no compromising of the sorts of things that can be thought; a commitment to publishing powerful cutting-edge scholarship; *but* a conviction that these things are essentially communicable, that we can find a language that is enterprising, individual and shareable.

To achieve this we need a form that can capture the genuine challenge and vigour of thinking. Shakespeare is intellectually exciting, and so too are the ideas and debates that thinking about his work can provoke. But published scholarship often fails to communicate much of this. It is difficult to sustain excitement over the 80–120,000 words customary for a monograph: difficult enough for the writer, and perhaps even more so for the reader. Scholarly articles have likewise become a highly formalized mode not only of publication, but also of intellectual production. The brief length of articles means that a concept can be outlined, but its implications or application can rarely be tested in detail. The decline of sustained, exploratory attention to the singularity of a play's language, occasion, or movement is one of the unfortunate results. Often 'the play' is somehow assumed, a known and given thing that is not really worth exploring. So we spend our time pursuing collateral contexts: criticism becomes a belated, historicizing footnote.

Important things have got lost. Above all, any vivid sense as to why we are bothered with these things in the first place. Why read? Why go to plays? Why are they important? How does any pleasure they give relate to any of the things we labour to say about them? In many ways, literary criticism has forgotten affective and political immediacy. It has assumed a shared experience of the plays and then averted the gaze from any such experience, or any testing of it. We want a more ductile and sensitive mode of production; one that has more chance of capturing what people are really thinking and reading about, rather than what the pre-empting imperatives of journal or respectable monograph tend to encourage.

Furthermore, there is a vast world of intellectual possiblity – from the past and present – that mainstream Shakespeare criticism has all but ignored. In recent years there has been a move away from 'theory' in literary studies: an aversion to its obscure jargon and complacent self-regard; a sense that its tricks were too easily rehearsed and that the whole game has become one of diminishing returns. This has further encouraged a retreat into the supposed safety of historicism. Of course the best such work is stimulating, revelatory, and indispensable. But too often there is little trace of any struggle; little sense that the writer is coming at the subject afresh, searching for the most appropriate language or method. Alternatively, the prose is so labored that all trace of an urgent story is quite lost.

We want to open up the sorts of thinking – and thinkers – that might help us get at what Shakespeare is doing or why Shakespeare matters. This might include psychology, cognitive science, theology, linguistics, phenomenology, metaphysics, ecology, history, political theory; it can mean other art forms such as music, sculpture, painting, dance; it can mean the critical writing itself becomes a creative act.

In sum, we want the minigraphs to recover what the Renaissance 'essay' form was originally meant to embody. It meant an 'assay' – a trial or a test of something; putting something to the proof; and doing so in a form that is not closed-off and that cannot be reduced to a system. We want to communicate intellectual activity at its most alive: when it is still exciting to the one doing it; when it is questing and open, just as Shakespeare is. Literary criticism – that is, really thinking about words in action, plays as action – can start making a much more creative and vigorous contribution to contemporary intellectual *life*.

Simon Palfrey and Ewan Fernie

Act 1

Shakespeare Behind Bars: *Julius Caesar* at Luther Luckett Correctional Complex

It's 18 May 2004 at the Luther Luckett Correctional Complex in LaGrange, Kentucky. For many at Luckett, a medium-security men's prison with an inmate population comprised primarily of rapists, drug offenders and murderers, it's just another day in the big house. But for the members of Shakespeare Behind Bars (SBB), who gradually file into the prison chapel, their meeting place, this is the day they've spent nine months preparing for: the premiere of their production of *Julius Caesar*.

Founded in 1995 by Artistic Director Curt Tofteland, SBB is an acting company in which inmates perform unaltered, full-length Shakespearean plays as they appear in the First Folio. Tofteland developed the program in order to offer inmates an outlet for artistic expression and as a tool for learning literacy and social skills such as tolerance and conflict resolution. At the same time, the program is meant to function as a safe forum in which violent offenders are able come to terms with their pasts – a process which frequently involves the inmates acknowledging crimes and abuses they themselves suffered in childhood as well as taking responsibility for their own violent acts as teenagers and adults – through the experiences of identification, role-playing and catharsis.

Unfortunately, the final dress rehearsal of *Julius Caesar* is getting off to a rocky start. Two of the show's stars, Sammie Byron, who plays Brutus, and DeMond Bush, who plays Antony, announce that they may need to leave at any moment to participate in an outreach program for at-risk youth. On top of that, Ron Brown, who plays Cassius, hasn't shown up yet. Rumor has it that he's 'still in the mess hall' and expected to be late again. Regardless, Tofteland decides to run the scenes that involve most of the company, Caesar's murder and Mark Antony's speech, and he responds to his actors with a mixture of defiance and humor.

'Okay, we're going to do the assassination,' Curt barks out. 'Leonard, you stand in for Ron. Come on, now! Where are my killers? I need my killers!'

'That's a loaded question,' one of the inmates jokes back.

'Yeah! Be careful who you're calling a killer,' says another, straightfaced.

The murder of Caesar, Tofteland reminds the group, is supposed to be performed in slow motion. The conspirators are supposed to breathe in and out heavily, as if they're possessed. After a series of collective stabs, the men are supposed to hold up their wooden knives and release the attached red paper streamers, which are meant to represent the blood flowing from Caesar's body. Following that, they're supposed to put on red gloves to signify that they've washed their hands in Caesar's blood.

'You're wolves. You're a wolf pack. You're on the hunt for blood,' Curt tells them. But most of the men seem unable to pretend to be bloodthirsty wolves, let alone to get the red streamers to unfurl from their wooden knives at the right time.

'Dammit,' says one man, throwing his hands up in frustration. 'Curt, I can't get my stupid knife to work.' Tofteland says, 'That's okay, Stone. Just hold your streamer in your other hand if you're not coordinated enough. Find your own way to solve the problem. You don't have to be like everyone else. Just do it to the best of your ability.'

And then Tofteland turns to the group. 'Guys, listen up. The goal is not perfection. Shakespeare Behind Bars is about the journey. Stay in the moment. Work with what you have. Be truthful to your characters when you're onstage. That's all you need to do.

Remember what Hamlet says, "Hold as 'twere the mirror . . ."' Tofteland's voice trails off. 'What does Hamlet say?' he prompts the men. Two or three of the inmates look down in the ground in concentration and whisper to themselves, 'Hold as 'twere the mirror up to nature.'

'Just tell the truth,' Curt instructs. 'That's all you need to do; just tell the truth.'

As the conspirators rehearse the assassination scene, other members of the group buzz around the chapel, busily rearranging the plastic chairs into rows on each of the four sides of the room to mark out their makeshift stage. Every now and then someone darts a glance at me out of the corner of his eye. 'Who's she?' I hear one inmate ask.

'I don't know, man,' says his friend, 'But I'm glad she's here.'

'Curt told us she's a Shakespeare professor,' replies another member of the acting troupe.

'Nah,' says the first. 'She looks too young to be a professor.' I ignore the men's whispers and try to pretend that I'm not nervous, but the truth is I've been so scared I haven't been able to sleep for the past three nights. This is my first time in a prison. I walk around the room, snapping photos, as the men prepare the stage.

From the time I was in high school, my father has volunteered at the city jail several days a week, befriending the inmates, assisting them financially and providing odd jobs after their release to help them 'get back on their feet.' On at least one occasion, he hired an ex-offender to care for my family's front lawn. I still have memories of my mother coming home from work and telling my father, 'Gordon, that guy with the mower had better not be one of your jailbirds!' and of my father and me driving by a man sitting on a country bridge with a paper grocery bag and my dad saying, 'There's my buddy Duane! Oh no, it looks like he's off the wagon again.' But if you had told me, back when I was a teenager, that I would be visiting a prison myself one day, I would have laughed at you. And I never in a million years would I have thought that I'd be going to prison to see, of all things, a Shakespeare play.

In fact, the notion of Shakespeare as a disciplinary and educational tool in secure settings is not a new one. According to Marianne Montgomery, playbills and newsletters at the Folger Shakespeare Library indicate that Shakespeare was performed in US prisons as far back as the American Civil War, and Niels Herold has found evidence from a travel narrative that *Hamlet* was performed by impressed seamen (that is to say, an incarcerated company of actors) on an English ship in 1607, in what just might be the first performance of secure-setting Shakespeare. Moreover, a number of Shakespearean actors have visited prisons and asylums including the nineteenth century actress Ellen Terry, who visited mental hospitals in preparation for her performance of Ophelia (Melville). Finally, imprisoned black Americans from Malcolm X to Don King have taught themselves Shakespeare during their incarcerations. 'Jail was my school,' King has said, of the four years he spent in prison for manslaughter. 'I read Aristotle and Homer. I got into Sigmund Freud. When I dealt with William Shakespeare, I got to know him very well as a man. I love Bill Shakespeare. He was some bad dude. Intellectually, I went into jail with a peashooter and came out armed with a nuclear bomb' (Hauser).

While prison Shakespeare is not an entirely new phenomenon, the 1980s and 1990s were especially remarkable in that a significant number of prison Shakespeare programs were initiated by professors and theatre directors across the country. Just a few years before Curt Tofteland founded Shakespeare Behind Bars in Kentucky, Jean Trounstine established a theatre group at the Framingham Women's Prison in Massachusetts. At around the same time, Agnes Wilcox created the Prison Performing Arts Project in Missouri – she now runs programs in both men's and women's prisons, as well as offering workshops for teenagers. And in Indiana, Laura Bates, who has been doing prison Shakespeare work for more than 25 years, developed a Shakespeare group for inmates in solitary confinement at Wabash Valley Correctional Facility, called Shakespeare in the SHU. More recently, in 2005, Jonathan Shailor began the

Shakespeare Project at Racine Correctional Institution in Wisconsin with a full-length production of *King Lear*.

These are only some of the secure-setting Shakespeare programs. There are others, in England, for instance, like Shakespeare Comes to Broadmoor, organized in the 1980s by psychotherapist Murray Cox, dramatherapist Sue Jennings and the Royal Shakespeare Company (RSC). In addition to the Broadmoor troupe, the London Shakespeare Workout Prison Project, registered as an official charity in 2002, conducts workshops in Her Majesty's Prisons Bedford, Feltham, Lewes, Lowdham Grange, The Mount and Woodhill. RSC voice coach Cicely Berry has been involved with prison Shakespeare since 1984 when she worked with Paul Schoolman on a *Julius Caesar* film adaptation at HMP Dartmoor (p. 199). Jessica Saunders, dramatherapist at HMP Holloway, England's largest prison for women, and her theatre company have written and performed various Shakespeare spin-offs including a *Hamlet* adaptation entitled *The Tragedy of Ophelia* (p. 221). There are also Shakespeare programs in the US for at-risk youth and juvenile offenders, such as Will Power to Youth, which is put on by the Los Angeles Shakespeare Festival; Incarcerated Youth at Play, founded by the Actors' Shakespeare Company in Cambridge, Massachusetts; and Shakespeare in the Courts, run by Shakespeare and Company of Lennox, Massachusetts.

When it comes to mission objectives, many prison Shakespeare directors perceive their programs as being primarily educational, providing inmates with a venue for improving literacy and social skills, and cultivating artistic talent. Others regard Shakespeare as a spiritual force. Judge Paul Perachi, who founded the Shakespeare in the Courts program, believes that Shakespeare has a special kind of 'inexplicable magic' when it comes to Corrections. In his estimation of the power of Shakespeare's verse to touch and transform criminals' lives, Perachi is not alone. Indeed, many *inmates* themselves consider Shakespeare to be a moralizing force, and not just any moralizing force, but the best and sometimes the only option after other methods, including religion and institutional surveillance, have failed. Chris Johnston, a theatre director who often works in prisons, says that prison drama programs are successful because they 'set up a kind of parallel universe where experiences as profound as those of both the offender and the victim can be explored. Participants can begin to experience some kind of victim empathy because they recognize the intensity and compulsion of the drives which make them want to offend. By linking these different kinds of experiences within the same aesthetic spectrum we can start to reduce the sense which many offenders have which is that of operating alone, in a void where [their] actions make no difference in the social world' (p. 134). According to Mark Rylance, who played Hamlet in the first RSC performance at Broadmoor, 'Any play if it is done well, and particularly a Shakespeare play, breaks down our conceptions of the limitations of human beings. You *can* change. You *can* be something different' (p. 34).

Back at the *Julius Caesar* rehearsal, many of the men in the Shakespeare Behind Bars company seem to have become so adept at changing their lives that they're having a hard time pretending (or remembering, in some cases) what it's like to be a killer. After rehearsing Caesar's assassination several times in a row, it's still not working. By this time Ron Brown has arrived and stepped into his role of Cassius. When Tofteland reminds the actors that they need to dramatize their thought processes rather than just stab Caesar and walk back to their original marks as nothing has happened, Brown, who looks like the long lost twin of gangsta rapper Ja Rule, offers some unsolicited advice to his colleagues.

'Excuse me. The problem is we know all this. Curt done said it, like, eight million times. It still depends on us; he's not gonna be out there. And so you have to think, you know, you gotta pay attention to what's going on. We're acting. We're portraying killing somebody, so we can't back up like, "Okay, I know I'm supposed to move here." You just stabbed somebody, several times, so you gotta try to think like that.'

And then Brown's tone grows even more scolding. Someone has been messing with his props. How is he supposed to play Cassius if people are always snatching his gloves? 'If the props and stuff in there ain't yours, do not mess with it! Simple as that. Don't mess with it.'

Across the room, Jerry Guenthner seconds Brown's complaint. 'Put your stuff where you want it. And if it ain't yours, you ain't put it there, don't touch it! If I come out for this scene without my sword again, there's gonna be hell to pay.'

Jerry Guenthner's knickname Big G is well deserved. He's about six feet, five inches tall and weighs 275 pounds. When he threatens the other actors, I don't know whether to laugh or run for the door. In any case, I'm pretty sure that the prison production of *Julius Caesar* is on a one-way train to Disasterville. There's no way they'll be ready for this evening's performance.

And then DeMond Bush enters the arena, cradling the body of Caesar in his arms as he walks about the stage. At first I'm impressed with his strength. I've never seen one man carry another man before, and DeMond does it with such gentleness and ease, as if the man he's holding weighs no more than a child. DeMond kneels down on the ground, holding Caesar in a *pietá* pose before laying him on the ground and climbing into the pulpit. It's actually a step ladder that DeMond ascends, but it might as well be a pulpit. I feel like I've been transported back in time, like the prison chapel has just become Dexter Avenue First Baptist Church, like I'm listening to Reverend King. 'Friends, Romans, Countrymen,' DeMond announces with outstretched arms. I lend him my ears. DeMond is captivating, breathtaking, enchanting. The words may be Shakespeare's but the rhythm and cadence are straight out of a black Baptist seminary. 'Read the will!' the men shout at DeMond. 'Yeah, read the will!' I want to say.

After the rehearsal, DeMond approaches me with a smile.

'Is this your first time in prison?' he asks.

'Yes,' I say. What gave it away?

'Are you scared?' he asks, empathetically.

'No,' I tell him, 'No, I'm okay.' And I am.

That evening a miracle happens. No one forgets a single line. Stone unfurls his streamer in perfect time. Ron's gloves are right where they should be. The chairs lining the walls are no longer empty; they're filled with fellow inmates. Not a man in the house laughs when Hal Cobb, who plays Portia, embraces and caresses Sammie Byron. No one scoffs at the red streamers during the assassination scene. When DeMond displays Caesar's bloody mantle, a white gauzy sheet with a dozen or so streamers attached, walking around and holding it in front of each audience member with tears of anger in his eyes, they look back at him with sorrow. The men jump to their feet at the end of the play, clapping and whistling enthusiastically.

During the talkback session after the show, the inmates in the audience tell the Shakespeare Behind Bars actors, 'Thank you so much for doing this.'

'I want to commend you,' says one man, 'That was fantastic. I think I might need to get involved in your program.' Another inmate, who looks to be in his 60s, stands and addresses the younger members of the group. 'Since you've been in Shakespeare, I've seen you change. We've all seen you change. You've grown. And I'm proud of you.' The Shakespeare Behind Bars actors tease a third man, pointing out that he's never missed any of their performances. 'You're our biggest fan. We're grateful for your support. But there's no need to cry,' they tell him. The man has tears streaming down his face. 'Well, that's real. That's heartfelt,' he smiles between his sniffles. 'I love you guys.'

The next evening, another performance of the play is staged in the Visitor's Room for an audience that includes the men's families and various teachers and theatre practitioners in the local area. Unlike the chapel, which feels warm and inviting, the Visitor's Room, with its white concrete floors and cement block walls, resembles an undersized cafeteria in an old elementary school building. The signs taped to the doors and windows remind the inmates and their families that any displays of affection are strictly regulated. 'Physical contact with an inmate shall be limited only to a brief hug and kiss at the beginning and conclusion of the visit,' reads one poster. 'Only infants (children under one year old) may be held by inmate. All other children must be seated or held by visiting parent or guardian,' reads another. 'You're saying that if a man has a two-year-old son, for instance, he's not allowed to hold him on his lap?' I ask Karen Heath, the Shakespeare Behind Bars staff liaison. 'Yep,' Karen replies, 'those are the rules.'

'But what if the child reaches out for his father to hold him?' I ask.

'The inmates have to tell their kids no; they can't hold them,' she insists. 'Those are the rules.'

By the end of the second day, I've met several of the lead actors. As they come through the door that leads from the prison yard to the Visitors' Room, they all say hello. DeMond approaches me with outstretched arms, Big G collects an embrace, and then an Shakespeare Behind Bars participant I have never met comes up and stands right in front of me. He says nothing. 'Hi,' I say, offering my hand. He politely shakes my hand. But he still stands in front of me. Finally he raises his arms up. I give him a quick hug, and he nods his head in satisfaction, turns around and walks away. 'That's Jason Wheeler,' DeMond whispers to me. 'He doesn't say much; he's really shy. It took a lot of guts for him to come up to you.' When I look up from my notebook again, there's a group of three or four men next to my chair, standing one behind the other. 'Look out, now. Here come the damn hug line,' Ron Brown mutters under his breath, with the same dry sense of humor that informs his performance of Cassius. Shane Williams, a tall, handsome man in his twenties, keeps coming up to me and then walking away. During future visits, Shane and I will joke about one of my colleague's reactions when she sees my photos of the *Julius Caesar* production: 'Is it just my imagination, or could he be a male model?' she swoons, pointing at Shane. But for now, Shane has something more important to say. He wants to tell me how much the Shakespeare program means to him, but will I please shut the tape recorder off? I turn off the recorder and smile at him. Shane tries to speak, but his eyes well up with tears, and he waves me off. 'I'll talk to you later, girl,' he says. 'I'll tell you later.'

Soon the visitors begin arriving. When Curt brings in his wife, Marcia Tofteland, a multiple sclerosis sufferer, the men flock to the side of her wheelchair, including the normally taciturn Brown. Just the evening before, following the performance on the yard, Brown had collected donations for the Muscular Dystrophy Association from his fellow inmates, most of whom make 85 cents a day. All of the men had immediately reached into their pockets to contribute, pulling out bill after bill. A week's salary in one case. A month's salary in another. As I watch them on bended knee around Marcia's wheelchair, I understand why. They love her. After all the visitors have arrived and the play is about to begin, Curt announces that there will be a slight delay. The security-controlled door leading from the hallway into the Visitors' Room is broken and won't shut. A couple of inmate electricians are called upon to repair the faulty wiring. As one holds the ladder and the other climbs up it, screwdriver and pliers in hand, Marcia leans her head toward me and says, 'How ironic that the inmates are fixing the door that keeps them locked in.'

As I circulate around the room during intermission, I hear references to Shakespeare in almost every conversation. 'When are we going to get you into a dress?' the men tease Jerry Guenthner. Big G has played Hamlet and Caliban, but is reluctant to play a woman because of his size. 'It would have to be a funny role in one of the comedies,' Big G insists, 'Probably the only way you'll see me in a dress is as Falstaff is we ever do *Merry Wives of Windsor*.' I pass DeMond Bush and hear him telling Ron Brown, 'Man, what you just said reminds me of Timon in *Timon of Athens*!' What's extraordinary about these conversations is that the Shakespeare Behind

Bars group has never performed *Merry Wives of Windsor* or *Timon of Athens*. And yet they can reel off lines and characters from every single Shakespeare play. The Shakespeare Behind Bars participants know Shakespeare better than many academics do.

During the question-and-answer session after the performance, a teacher in the audience remarks upon the inmates' extraordinary grasp of Shakespeare.

Having played Ariel in The Tempest, *Ryan 'Bulldog' Graham decided to take the smaller role of Trebonius in* Julius Caesar. Photo by Amy Scott-Douglass

'I've studied Shakespeare and I've read Shakespeare,' she says, 'but it almost seems that you have come to understand it so well that you almost live it. And I'm just wondering, are there lessons in Shakespeare that you really can feel that you're living?'

'Yes,' responds Richard Hughes, a Native American in his early 40s who plays Casca. 'Every time we get together to do another play, it's not so much a matter of us picking a role as we read through the script and a role grabs us. So I guess you as an audience would see that we do live through Shakespeare, but that's only because we reflect ourselves. In that way it lends an authenticity to the characters because each of us are resolving issues through Shakespeare. Through the art of theatre, Shakespeare helps us learn how to bettter cope with life on a day-to-day basis.'

Shane raises his hand. 'I don't really get into Shakespeare that much. I really think this stuff is kinda crazy,' he admits. But Curt said, "Hey, everybody in here has got a different reason for being in the program." And my reason . . . well, I was trying to explain this to Amy earlier, but I was getting choked up, and I can't handle all of that cryin' and stuff. But I was laying in my bed last night, thinking of everything that's going on. I've been locked up since I was 17. But my new discovery is for like three hours when we're doing a play, I've had this freedom. And it's freedom that you guys in the audience give us. And I ain't had that in a long time. And I thank you guys for coming and showing us love because without you guys there's no one.'

Following the talkback, the men are able to spend a few minutes chatting with their friends and family members, but the conservations are quickly interrupted by Karen Heath yelling at the inmates.

'Wrap it up, gentlemen!' she barks. 'Wrap it up *now*!'

Though Karen sounds like a bulldog, she gives me a look across the room as if to say that forcing families apart is her least favorite part of being involved with the Shakespeare program. 'Hey,' she seems to say to me, 'I'm just doing my job.'

It's a quarter to nine. The men will be punished if they are not back in their cells in 15 minutes for the third and final count of the day. But before they can go back onto the yard, each man has to go through a cavity search. The men have only a few minutes to say goodbye to loved ones and guests. One of the officers, less enlightened than Karen, walks around the room, snapping the plastic glove on his right hand.

As the visitors leave out one door, the actors are corralled into a small, glassed corridor – it's a chamber, really – where each man will wait to be strip-searched. First Ron walks in, then Shane, then Big G, then Sammie, then Richard, then DeMond. But as soon as they're inside the glassed corridor, the men turn their backs on the door leading to the examination area and look back into the Visitor's Room, their theatre, waving and smiling at Curt, Marcia, Michelle and me. From behind the glass walls, the men begin chanting the name of Curt's wife. 'Mar-cia! Mar-cia! Mar-cia! Mar-cia!' they say again and again, smiling at her and gently pounding their fists in the air. It is the most extraordinary moment I've ever witnessed in my life. I look at Marcia. She has tears streaming down her face, which, because of her paralysis, she cannot wipe away.

'It's a tradition they started many years ago,' she tells me. 'They always do this for me.'

'Would you like me to take you up to the windows so that you can say goodbye to them up close?' I ask.

Marcia smiles and nods. I wheel her over in front of the men. From behind the glass, they blow kisses and clasp their hands to their hearts.

'I love you!' each man calls out to Marcia. 'I love you!'

As the men disappear from view, one by one, the chanting grows softer until there are no more men left.

'Time to go,' Curt says quietly, and I wheel Marcia away from the empty room.

'Shakespeare is my Church': Criminality and the Discourse of Conversion

If Jerry Guenthner were one of Snow White's Seven Dwarves, he'd be Happy. He has Happy's twinkling eyes and rosy cheeks. He also has Happy's tummy, although, as he proudly tells me, he lost 75 pounds in 2003, the same year that he played Caliban in the Shakespeare Behind Bars production of *The Tempest*. Imprisoned since 1986 for killing a undercover police officer during a drug bust, Big G, I am told, is nothing like the 'defiant, angry' man who stood in front of the judge decades ago. While Big G might pretend to threaten his fellow castmates when they mess around with his stage properties, especially his favorite wooden sword, he is the epitome of kindness with me. He is also the most enthusiastic fan of William Shakespeare I've ever met.

'The thing that's so mind-boggling,' Big G tells me 'is that Shakespeare's writings, 400 and some years ago, reflect our lives and everything we go through. It's just amazing. It's awesome. It's fantastic. I remember being exposed to it in high school, reading a little Shakespeare, and it's horrible to read. You should read it aloud or go see it.'

'What did you read in high school?' I ask. Big G can't even recall.

'Probably *Romeo and Juliet*,' he responds. 'Probably for English 102 class or something. I played football the whole time that I was in high school, and I used to say, "God, Shakespeare? You've got to be kidding! No way." And now I'm here doing it, and it's taken up so much of my life. Shakespeare has changed my entire outlook on everything that is everything.'

I tell Big G that I heard his performance of Caliban was a big hit when Shakespeare Behind Bars toured to the nearby women's prison, Kentucky Correctional Institute for Women.

He blushes. 'They did love me. I guess I stole, like, every scene. They loved the monster; they sure enough did. It was very flattering.'

I ask him what it was like to play Hamlet in 2002, a part he had to lobby for against the three other key Shakespeare Behind Bars players – DeMond, Sammie and Ron.

'To do Hamlet was so overwhelming that it almost took over my life,' he says. 'I had to spend each day working on my lines, and when I would do work in the laundry over in the dorms. So I've got one load in the washer, one in the dryer, and I'm just sitting there, "Alas, poor Yorick, I knew him well."'

Leonard Ford, who plays Lucius in *Julius Caesar* and whose past roles include Claudius and Tamora, tells me that he had a similar unfamiliarity with Shakespeare in high school.

'I'd never really known much Shakespeare before I came to prison, other than the little bit you do in high school English class.'

'Did you like it in high school?' I ask.

'No,' Leonard says, but he certainly was willing to use Shakespeare to, as Robin Williams' character puts it in *Dead Poets' Society*, 'woo women.'

'When I was a senior in English,' Leonard remembers, 'we read *Hamlet* and I was in the drama department, so the teacher had me read Hamlet, and I picked up a girl in the class because she thought I had a great voice. I mean, it worked out, you know what I'm saying? It was nice. And I *liked* her, too! But as far as *Hamlet* goes, I didn't have a clue what was going on.'

'Why Shakespeare?' I ask him. 'Intellectually and philosophically? Why Shakespeare? I mean, why not Thorton Wilder?'

Leonard tells me that there are two reasons for preferring Shakespeare: the beauty of the language and the challenge of comprehension.

'Just hearing the words trip off the tongue and the sounds that are made . . . it's very beautiful to me. That's what draws me in. Then you have the obstacle of understanding content. With Shakespeare you can extract from the text or you can read into it. It's like the text has a life of its own, and I have never experienced that with modern plays, with the Wilders or the Inges or the O'Neills or the Ionescos.'

'You knew right away that Shakespeare Behind Bars was for you?' I ask.

Leonard's voice lowers and softens. 'Yes, because for me what is so horrible about prison is intellectual and psychologically it shuts you down. I mean, there's a very real connection between being caged in physically and caged in mentally, very real.'

I don't think I could find two people more different than Leonard Ford and Howard Ralston. When I meet with Leonard – a slim, tidy, white man who enjoyed a well-paying job in the business sector before his imprisonment – he's just come from yoga. Before that he was reading Eastern philosophy. Before that he was writing a treatise against narrow-minded conceptions of masculinity. Before that he was practicing Spanish guitar. Howard Ralston, on the other hand, a huge African-American man, endured a life on the streets, the kind of life where you have to shoot, according to Howard, in self-defense. He doesn't do yoga. He doesn't read philosophy. He doesn't play the guitar. But when it comes to Shakespeare, Howard has a grace and wisdom all his own. He lays it on the line for me.

'I will say it like this. Shakespeare was before his time. Shakespeare still lives even though he's dead. His spirit lives on. A lot of things that he wrote are happening in the world today, and we can relate to some of it. When I was a youngster, I used to go see it in the park, but I had no desire to be involved in no kind of Shakespeare acting or none of that. Only when I got here, I seen a few plays, and Big G and me, you know, we've always been real cool. He said, "Man, you wanna join Shakespeare, man?" I said, "Man, I don't know how to do that stuff." He said, "Man, you can do it. Sure you can." And I'm like, "Man, I don't know, man." He said, "Well, just come up here with me and check it out and see if you like it." So I did. And they gave me a small role, 'cause that's all I wanted at the time, 'cause I didn't want to take nothing on big not never doin' it before. Then I began to like it. Some of the plays have a lot to do with what's going on in the world today. And Shakespeare is a good program, and I enjoy all the plays that there are.'

Having said that, Howard's not ready to limit his repertoire to the early modern canon.

'Shakespeare is not the only play that I will do. You know, if I was out, and there was a theatre doing newer plays, I'd probably try to get some kind of action in on that. It don't have to be about just Shakespeare, but Shakespeare's my number one choice. This is what I've done for, like, four years.'

Marcel Herriford, Howard's counterpart, agrees. Marcel's performance as Miranda may have won rave reviews from his peers, as well as helped him come to terms with his relationship with his father, a 'controlling white man' reminiscent of Prospero, according to Marcel, who grew up with his African-American mother. But unlike some Luckett inmates, Marcel is keeping his theatrical options open.

He rolls his eyes when asked about his more bardalotrous colleagues.

'A lot of the guys, Sammie and Big G and them, are always reading other Shakespeare plays and books on Shakespeare. They're really serious about this Shakespeare. They will talk Shakespeare 24 hours, seven days a week, which I won't. I will leave them when they speak to Shakespeare 24/7. I say, "Well, okay, I'm gone because I have another life besides Shakespeare."'

Floyd Vaughn, who plays Caesar, is one of Big G's most loyal converts to the Shakespeare program. A 45-year-old Texan with sparkling blue eyes and the word 'murder' inked on his arm, a tattoo that looks like an inside job from decades ago, Vaughn doesn't wait for me to ask any questions. The first thing out of his mouth when he enters the interview room is, 'Man, I love this play!' I laugh and ask him to tell me about how he got involved in the program.

'I used to hate Shakespeare,' Vaughn says, shaking his head as if he can't believe he ever made such a huge mistake. 'But that was because I didn't understand him. I was ignorant to the fact of what he actually was saying. Big G, my roommate, was always quoting Shakespeare. And I would just look at him and say, "Why are you doing that? I have no idea what you're talking about." He was constantly quoting one thing after another in every single conversation that we had. Like, say you're sitting here. He'll walk in and start talking Shakespeare to you. And I was thinking, well, why won't he just talk to me normal, you know? And it was turning me off. I was hating it. Well, as time went by, I starting picking up the book every now and then. He'd quote it, and then after he'd leave I'd look it up.'

I chuckle at the idea of inmates lining their rooms with copies of Shakespeare. But Vaughn is serious. 'Do you have a copy of Shakespeare's works in your dorm?' I ask him.

'Yes, ma'am,' he says. 'I got the Arden edition, I have *Shakespeare for Dummies*, I have two dictionaries, and Guenther has several Shakespeare books, too. So with all the books that we have, if there's any problem we go straight to the books.'

Vaughn continues his story. '*Julius Caesar* is what got me involved. Back in 2001, Jerry Guenther and Sammie Byron were doing one of the skits where Brutus and Cassius go at it inside their tent, and they was doin' it in the bullpen. And it was so good that . . . I can't put it into words. Everybody on the walkway just stopped and just watched the whole process. And I was just stunned by what they did. And I thought, "Wow." And as soon as they seen me, sitting there, and I clapped for them when they was done, they said, "Bingo. We got you."'

'I'll tell you something else Shakespeare's done for me,' Vaughn continues. 'It's helped me be able to talk to people. Before, like talking to you now? I couldn't talk to you at all. I was afraid that you was gonna judge me. Like you're a superior person. You're a professor, you know, and I would be intimidated more than anything. But I've met quite a few people through Curt's project, and they're awesome people. And I think that what I like about them is when they come in here they don't stick their nose up and think they're better because they're out there and I'm a criminal. All my life, especially when I came in here, I've always thought that people on the outside were going to think of me as a piece of dirt. Some of them do, and that's okay: I've made my bed, and I've got to sleep in it. But when I started Shakespeare, I was in awe of the fact that total strangers could come in here and treat me like I was somebody. Like, last night, when Guenther's mother come over and hugged me at intermission, I almost cried. She's good people. And she reminded me so much of my mom before she died; I had to turn my back because I was gonna cry. Like I'm getting ready to do now. I've got to quit talking about it or I'll start crying, ma'am.

But it's too late. Vaughn's eyes well up with tears. He reaches behind me to a stack of paper towels which he uses as a handkerchief. When Leonard sees that Vaughn has been crying, Leonard smiles compassionately. He understands why Shakespeare provides Vaughn an emotional outlet that no other prison program offers.

'It is very difficult in prison to find a group where men are willing to be supportive of one another,' Leonard explains. 'Support and personal growth and reward for accepting responsibility are not part of most programs in prison. They are certainly not part of the normal way the prison bureaucracy is run. Shakespeare Behind Bars is different from the daily routine of prison; it's the opposite.'

Hal Cobb confirms Leonard's assessment of the prison administration. 'We are not treated with that amount of respect and humanity by a good majority of the staff and the other inmates. But people like Curt and most of the college teachers around here are not Corrections employees, and they've got a different perspective, and they're here to help us change our lives and give us opportunities to change ourselves.'

When the inmates describe their experiences with Shakespeare, many of them employ an undeniably religious discourse. Howard speaks of Shakespeare in the same kind of language that might be used to describe Jesus Christ, ascribing divine qualities to Shakespeare, characterizing him as immortal, his spirit living on even though his body is dead, and this depiction of Shakespeare as divine and of the Shakespeare program as a spiritual experience is only amplified by the fact that many of the rehearsals and performances are held in the prison chapel. New initiates like Marcel talk about veteran Shakespeareans like Sammie and Big G as though they were zealous devouts, Shakespearean monks, lining their cells with books, quoting from plays as if they were scripture and witnessing to men on the yard in an effort to bring others to Shakespeare. 'Shakespeare has changed my entire outlook on everything that is everything,' Big G says. 'I can see redemption in the distance,' Richard says. This is the discourse of conversion.

It seems to me that there are two reasons the discourse of conversion is so prevalent in Shakespeare Behind Bars. The first reason is that there is a spiritual component to the Shakespeare program. The men speak about Shakespeare as a divine force because, quite simply, Shakespeare has touched their hearts and souls. Many of the men are quick to point out that they are 'spiritual but not religious.' Shakespeare aligns with their spirituality in that they regard Shakespeare as a sort of secular redeemer, a savior who is tolerant and loving and accepting of everyone. As Marcel puts it, 'Shakespeare is like a god to a lot of the other guys here, because the majority of them don't believe in a god. They believe in sort of . . . like . . . revolution.'

For Hal Cobb, who was raised in a restrictive, fundamentalist Baptist home, the Shakespeare program functions as a substitute church. A preacher's kid and former music minister himself, Hal murdered his wife by dropping a hairdryer into her bathtub after she told him that she was pregnant with their second child.

'Shakespeare is *my* church. Shakespeare *is* my church,' Hal says. 'The chapel offerings here do not meet my personal needs. I'm not welcome in most of the services.'

'Why?' I ask.

'Because I'm gay,' he replies. 'I don't hide it anymore. I hid it for 30 years, and my wife is dead because I hid it and couldn't deal with it and felt God had turned his back on me. There's no excuse for my actions but, to me, that's why it happened. Most of the church volunteers who come in come from very evangelical backgrounds. They'll go up to the chapel, and they're talking anti-everything.'

Hal wags his finger in impersonation of the prison missionaries. 'If it's in black and white in the scripture, it's got to be true. Homosexuality is one of the greatest sins.'

'They're constantly bashing it,' Hal complains, 'although many of the ones who attend up there, after bashing for awhile, are the ones who are wanting to try to get a little action on the side when they think nobody's looking, which never happens around here – everybody knows what everybody's doing; there are no secrets.'

'How is Shakespeare a church to you?' I ask Hal. 'Why is Shakespeare a welcoming place when church isn't?'

Hal explains, 'Curt insists on personal responsibility and telling the truth. Those are kind of the benchmarks of the program. And he makes no excuses for any of the things that we've done to get here. Curt's the only one who's ever said to me, "You're responsible for two people's lives. If you've taken somebody's life, you have to live for their life and for your life now." And no one else has ever said that. You would think that would be what the prison environment should be about anyway – accountability and people holding you responsible – but that's not the case. My experience is that prison is not at all about rehabilitation and change. It's warehousing. It's warehousing human waste. Shakespeare is the opposite of that. And, really, everything in the way Curt has us work with Shakespeare just resounds with my own spiritual journey.'

Although Luckett's chaplain, Mark Wessels, is not affiliated with the Shakespeare program, he certainly understands why so many inmates would be drawn to the Bard. 'Shakespeare approaches philosophical issues about how we live in society, how we order society, what a healthy relationship is, what boundaries we should maintain,' the chaplain says. 'These are issues that most of these guys didn't reflect on before they committed their crimes. Now that they're here, they're reflective, and many of them are repentant. Most of them wouldn't put their reflection and repentance into theological words, so I think that Shakespeare gives them a voice that perhaps they wouldn't have otherwise, a voice which I think definitely has a theological component to it.'

But at the same time that rituals such as repentance, confession, conversion, reformation and testimony are integral components of many religions, these very rituals are also part and parcel of the US trial system. When inmates come up before the parole board, their chances of being released depend upon not just saying that they've repented and reformed, but showing that they've repented and reformed. 'The only way you're gonna get out is if you can change and if you can demonstrate to other people that you've changed,' Big G tells me. 'They don't care. They'd just as soon warehouse you in here for the rest of your life. You need to change, and you need to show people that you can change and that you have changed.'

When it comes identifying the men who have experienced the most significant transformations during their tenure in the Shakespeare program, the Shakespeare Behind Bars participants mention two names in particular: DeMond Bush and Sammie Byron.

'When DeMond first got here, he was bad. He was *baaaad*,' says Vaughn, emphasizing the last word with his Southern drawl. Imprisoned since 1993 for a list of felonies, including drug possession, kidnapping and second-degree manslaughter, DeMond has been at Luckett since he was 18. Back in the 1990s, inmates were allowed to wear their own clothing, and DeMond took full advantage of the opportunity to fashion himself as a gangsta extraordinaire, dressing in hooded sweatshirts, wearing sunglasses indoors, and walking with a serious swagger. The men still take great delight in watching Curt 'do' his imitation of DeMond in the early days. 'But as he started growing up after being in the Shakespeare program,' explains Vaughn, 'Everybody could see the changes in him. It's no more "motherfuck this"; it's no more "motherfuck that."' Vaughn catches himself. 'I mean, every now and then he will say it,' Vaughn admits. 'You know, we're guys. And guys is gonna be guys. When there's no women around or somebody that you respect, things are going to be said. But otherwise from right now you would not know that DeMond was the same DeMond that he was eight or nine years ago. There's that much total difference.'

In Sammie Byron's case, his legendary Othello 'breakthrough' is probably the most celebrated moment in the history of the program.

As Sammie tells the story, the years of abuse – both verbal taunts about his mixed African-American and Mexican heritage, and sexual abuse by male relatives and friends – initiated a cycle of shame, sexual addiction and violent behavior. As an adult, Sammie became involved in extramarital affairs, including one with a woman named Carol. Day after day, Carol's threats to expose Sammie for an adulterer increased and their arguments became more and more violent. One evening, Carol threatened Sammie for the last time. He snapped, and strangled her to death. Sammie was sentenced to life in prison. By 1999, he had served almost 20 years, and he had, in many ways, established himself as what is frequently called 'a model prisoner.' He had taught himself to program computers, developed almost 200 software programs, and become the manager of the prison's computer lab – a lab which negotiated a six-figure contract with a major company. He had established himself as a star athlete, breaking the world record in weight-lifting by dead-lifting 760 pounds. But many prison administrators and employees were convinced that Sammie's rehabilitation was incomplete. Prison staff psychologist Julie Barto told Curt, 'I've spent hours and hours in therapy with Sammie. I know what he's done. He comes up for parole in 2003. And he's not ready yet.' And then, in 1999, Shakespeare Behind Bars performed *Othello*. Sammie cast himself in the title role expressly because he wanted to come to terms with his murder of Carol. The rehearsals of the scene in which Othello's strangles Desdemona were intense to say the least. Big G, one of Sammie's best friends, was there on the day of Sammie's epiphany.

'I remember the day when Sammie had his breakthrough up there in the Visitor's Room when we was rehearsing that scene. I mean, that play mirrored his crime to the point where it was just, like, identical, and I get goosebumps right now even just talking about it. And Mike Smith took the role of Desdemona because he knew that Sammie would need his support. I mean, we know each other and we're tight and we know that we're gonna find the truth in these characters and find it in our lives, and we knew there was gonna be a day when Sammie was gonna face that monster. And when all of it took place, I mean, Sammie broke down and . . .'

I interrupt. 'Describe that to me. What does that mean "broke down?"' I ask. 'Because I've seen Sammie cry – I've seen him cry in the play, during the talkbacks – but when Sammie Byron really breaks down, what does that mean?'

'Sammie, or any of us,' says Guenthner. 'You can cry and you can be emotional, but the pain and hurt that we've caused in peoples' lives and the mistakes that we've made no matter what you do you can't bring that person back and you can't undo the hurt that you did. The line I like best in *Hamlet* is "to hold as 'twere a mirror up to nature." And that's what we try to do. And when you look in that mirror and you find it relates really strongly to your past or your crime, that truth, that pain just comes out. And it's almost like a mental breakdown, such an emotional release that it's just, whew, it's a trip to watch.'

'Does that change a person's life, to have that kind of cathartic experience?' I ask.

Big G nods his head. 'It changes you. First of all, when you find that, some of the pain will go away. Your response that you have, your empathy that you have, all that will increase. And the truth, when you can touch it and you can let it out, it'll feel like a ton of bricks is off of you. The hardest thing for anybody in here to really get over is that you have to be able to forgive yourself. And it's really hard to do. I mean, I spent years trying to forgive myself and I had just come to a place where I needed to get past it. I can't bring my victim back, and so what can I do about it? I can lay down and let my life be worth nothing, or I can make a decision to change my life and make my life mean something. That's what a lot of us are trying to do.'

'There's a lot of men in prison that are not bad,' he continues. 'They just did bad things. And, as amazing as it seems, by experiencing Shakespeare and focusing on what Shakespeare wrote about 400 years ago and applying it in your life by either witnessing a character's mistakes and realizing why did he make those mistakes and if they mirrored your own life and what could you learn from them . . . or taking some of Shakespeare's more positive characters and seeing the traits that a positive character has and going, "Hey, I want those positive attributes in my life," you really can change. It's just an amazing transformation that you can undertake.'

Act 2

'Words Before Blows': Sammie Byron, Brutus

Whenever one of the inmates at Luckett comes up for parole, the prison staff, the leaders of the volunteer programs, and even his dearest friends caution him not to get his hopes up. Parole boards are tough. They're supposed to be tough. But in Sammie Byron's case, no one was worried. Yes, he had committed a crime of passion. Yes, he had been given a life sentence. But since then he had served 20 years. More importantly, he had truly changed. Prison staff psychologist Julie Barto had approached Curt Tofteland after witnessing Sammie's behavior after his Othello performance and said, '*Now* he's ready.' Even the most cynical prison guards referred to Sammie as the 'gentle giant.' If he was released and moved into their neighborhood, that'd be great with them; they'd be happy to lend a cup of sugar to someone as good and kind as Sammie. Yes, Sammie was sure to make parole. That's the way prison is supposed to work. You do the crime, you do the time, you get rehabilitated, and then you get to be released; you get to remember what it felt like to be free. One of the reasons Curt and the SBB members chose to produce *The Tempest* in 2003 was because of Prospero's 'Our revels now have ended' speech. They thought that they would be saying goodbye to their friend. *The Tempest* was supposed to mark Sammie's retirement from Shakespeare, or from SBB, at least.

It's 2004. And Sammie is still in prison.

I ask him how he's coping with the parole board's surprising decision. Sammie shakes his head. It hasn't been easy. He alternates between blaming the parole board and blaming himself.

'Everyone always says, "Sammie you've done all these good things. You're a good person." And everyone who knows me knows that I'm a good person. But then last year, when I went to the parole board I was given a six-year deferment – that's after doing 20 years. I thought, my God, I spent all afternoon talking about all the good things that I've done and all the achievements and accolades that's been given to me, but still it doesn't erase the crime that I commit-ted. Everyone thought that if anyone deserved to be out, it would be me, and they all said, "You are going to get out of prison," but the reality is I may not ever get out of prison, and it's because of the crime that I committed. I'm resolved to that, and I'm going to make the best of any situation that I'm in. The hardest thing was telling my family "Okay," you know, "I'm not getting out. I was denied parole. It didn't happen. It didn't happen this time, but I will get another chance in six more years."'

One year after the parole board's decision, Sammie still seems to be in shock. What more does he have to do to prove that he's a good man? 'You would think that, okay, you do all these things and then you will be rewarded,' Sammie says, shaking his head, 'but the reward sometimes is difficult to see.'

Nevertheless, Sammie has made a home for himself at Luckett. 'I'm friends with everyone,' he says. 'I get along with everyone, and I stay so busy. I work here as a computer programmer. All the jobs and everything that the data processing teams do, I create the soft-ware. I have created all of this. Never went to school for it, or anything, but took the time to learn it myself. So now we're work-ing two shifts. We have 120 men.'

'And you're in charge?'

'Yeah, I'm pretty much in charge,' he smiles. Sammie and his team key in public records data for Kentucky's Cabinet of Human Resources. They process marriage licenses, divorces, death certificates, educational surveys from the elementary schools, and surveys from the University of Kentucky. 'About two years ago they were about to shut the computer program down because they were worried about inmates having access to people's personal information,' says Sammie. 'So I created a snipet program – I can take any document and disguise it over 89 ways and only show you pieces of that document, so we got that program approved for the state, and now we can do any work because nobody can really see anything.'

'You taught yourself how to program computers?' I ask.

'Yes,' Sammie replies, and then he laughs at my stunned reaction. 'It's not that hard. Shakespeare was hard. Heck, Shakespeare is *still* hard.'

Having quickly segued to his favorite subject, Sammie tells me how important the Shakespeare program is to him. 'There's no experience like Shakespeare. It just encompasses all that life has to offer. There's nothing that's left out with Shakespeare, and you know when you think you have discovered everything in it, there's more in there. And I'm a testament, and our group is a testament, to the power of Shakespeare. I've been very fortunate while in prison. I've had some great counsellors and many years of treatment to get me to this point – and what Shakespeare has allowed me to do by inhabiting characters like Othello, Aaron, and even Proteus, is to see myself and to see how destructive I have been, the effect I have had on people. So, in a sense, role-playing these characters has really helped me to see myself. In *Julius Caesar*, I chose to play Brutus. I look at Brutus as a very sincere, good guy. He has great morals, great ethics, but he makes some really, really bad choices. Where I'm at in my life, we're pretty close in terms of honor and respect, but the difference between me and Brutus is I'm willing to wait to see what will happen, whereas Brutus is not willing to wait, and that is his mistake.'

I ask Sammie if his first introduction to Shakespeare came in prison with his performance as Proteus in the 1995 production of *Two Gentlemen of Verona*.

'No, of course not,' he says. 'I read Shakespeare in high school. *Romeo and Juliet*. Sammie scowls. 'I *read* it. Didn't *understand* it.'

'Hated it?' I suggest.

'Oh God, hated it!' he laughs. 'This don't make no sense at all,' Sammie says, impersonating a younger version of himself. 'But it turns out that *Romeo and Juliet* is a great story. With *Two Gents*, I had never heard of it. We went into that really just wanting to get through it. The guy who was Proteus backed out with about 30 days before the show, so I stepped up and performed Proteus. I think it was, like, 600 lines.'

'Was Othello the hardest role you played?' I ask him. Sammie immediately breaks into tears.

'Yeah, no doubt,' he replies.

'And it's not just because of the size of the role,' I say.

'No, no,' Sammie says, 'It has nothing to do with that.' He looks down at the floor and shakes his head. When he raises his head up again, the tears run down his face. I am more than a little surprised by Sammie's sudden, immediate reaction. As he sits in front of me crying, my first thought is that he's putting on a show, that his sorrow isn't sincere, only because I've never seen any human being break into tears so quickly.

'Will you talk to me about it?' I ask.

'Yeah, I'd be glad to talk to you about it.'

'Good.'

'Be a little bit patient,' he tells me.

'Sure,' I say.

And then Sammie wipes his tears from both eyes with one sweep of his massive hand, looks straight at me, and speaks. 'I can never get over this,' he says. 'And I don't try to fight it or hide it, and although it may look painful it's very liberating. I had to do . . . I had to do Othello . . . because it was so like the crime I committed, and it was not so much as to recreate the crime as it was to be sure that I understood it. My close friend Mike Smith played Desdemona. Even though he had his own insecurities to deal with in playing a woman's role. And so I got a chance to . . . I always wondered . . . no . . . it's very difficult to put yourself in the place of your victim, and in exploring Othello, it allowed me to in some sense recreate that moment. Then I was able to see, in the face of someone that I cared about, exactly what was going on with them. Very powerful. I already knew that what I did was not okay, but I needed to really understand the extreme pain that I caused, and that, in essence, motivates me to constantly be aware of how I treat others. People are so special and unique and important, and no matter what's going on, they don't deserve to be hurt in that fashion. Everything can always be worked out. There's always another way. There's no excuse for what I've done. I understand now. Like with Brutus, he doesn't take the time to give Caesar a chance, and I will never be like that. Never again.'

'Tell me what you did,' I encourage Sammie.

'I was married to a good woman. I had this extramarital relationship and it all come to an end, and I felt like I was going to be exposed, and then in a rage, I killed the woman I was having an affair with. It's just so insane in terms of how I processed things back then. I was just this bundle of pain. I didn't use drugs or drink or anything like that. Back then it was sex, and that's what I equated with making me feel good at the time.'

'What do you think of Mike, who played Desdemona?' I ask. 'Does it take a lot of guts for a guy to take the woman's part in a men's prison?'

'It takes a tremendous amount of courage for any man in here to play a woman's part. And of course just because Hal is gay doesn't mean that it's not as great a struggle for him even to play a female role. Mike did it for the group,' Sammie says. 'And . . . and . . .' Sammie breaks into tears again. 'And he did it for me.' Sammie chokes the words out between gasps for air.

'Did you ask him to play that role?'

'No. I think he just knew.' By this point Sammie is weeping, sobbing. 'He did it for me,' Sammie repeats, and the tone in his voice makes the statement sound like a question, like Sammie still can't believe someone loved him that much.

'It was almost like a divine intervention. Mike had so many in-securities himself, and for him to step up and take on such a role like that? It took tremendous courage. And trust. He trusted me. Before this group, I could never trust anyone with anything like that. I grew up in a very abusive background and had a lot of neglected needs. Love was something that was implied, but it was never shown; it was not demonstrated. And what this group is . . . what I learn and get to experience in this group is we can have some knock down, drag out fights and stuff, but we make up with love and that's something that's been absent in my life, and we say we're sorry, and it's more than that: it's meaningful because in saying that we're sorry, we take the time to express what it is we did, and so that communication is acknowledged. I was on the power-lifting team years ago over at KSR, Kentucky State Reformatory. I'm older now, but back then, I was the best in the state and one of the best in the world. In 1988, I broke the world record in the dead lift. I was ranked number one five years in a row. I used to be all this frustration and anger when I started to lift weights, and that's how I would express it . . . through that explosiveness. I had a gift; I was very strong. But then I had to move away from that into something different because just keeping it to myself was no good. I had to feel comfortable that I could argue without it turning into something ugly. I had to learn how to fight. And that it's okay to fight.'

As Sammie is talking, I realize that he has his *Julius Caesar* script in his hand. He's brought it with him to the interview. 'Is there a part that you can point to in your script, a particular line or speech that means something special to you?' I ask.

Sammie thinks about the question for a while. He flips through the pages. He wasn't expecting this question. 'Mostly I've just got my blocking notes or definitions in the margins,' he says, 'I haven't marked any personal passages.' And then he remembers. 'Oh yeah, the Cassius and Brutus scene!' he says, and he opens to Act 4. 'The Cassius and Brutus scene,' Sammie explains, 'makes me think about friendship and the importance of understanding that sometimes you can't always model people the way you want them to be, but they still have some uniqueness and this special quality in them that is important and admirable. At the very end when Cassius goes through the thing about

"Cassius is a weary of the world | Hated by the one he loves." That just stabs at me right there because essentially Cassius is saying to Brutus, "Can you accept me for who I am? Please accept me for who I am. It hurts so much when you reject me." And Cassius says, at the very end of that, "I that denied thee gold will give my heart." It's a scene about friendship and conflict resolution. They have a quarrel, but they don't kill each other. And both of them have valid reasons to be angry, and again, from this little scene, what's not said is that Brutus proclaims himself to be this honorable person, but at the same time, he knows where Cassius is getting his money. It's like accepting money from a drug dealer. It's dealing dirty. But that scene is just so ideal when you have just two friends right there who need each other, and then just accepting, "This is the way you are. I accept you for your faults.'"

Later that morning, after I have finished my first round of interviews and am walking toward the exit to get some lunch, Sammie comes up to me on the prison yard. 'Amy!' he says, 'I've found it!' He opens his *Julius Caesar* script and points to his favorite lines. 'See, right here. Cassius is angry, and Brutus is angry. They're both angry. But Brutus stops the fight. Brutus says, "Be angry when you will, it shall have scope; | Do what you will, dishonour shall be humour." And then Cassius says, "Give me your hand," and Brutus says, "And my heart too." Brutus stops the fight, you know? Brutus stops the fight.'

'He sure does,' I tell Sammie.

'Hey, if I don't see you this afternoon, I'll see you at the play tonight,' Sammie smiles. 'See you soon, though, okay?'

'See you soon, Sammie,' I say.

'Most Noble Brother, You Have Done Me Wrong': DeMond Bush, Mark Antony

After lunch, I can't get back to the prison fast enough. I've got three interviews scheduled for the afternoon, and my new favorite Shakespearean actor, DeMond Bush, is at the top of the list.

'Ask him to pronounce "Verona",' Sammie had told me. 'He can't do it! He can't do it, man! He says "Vanona". When we were in *Two Gents* together, we had to work with him on his diction constantly. We were like, "Come on, man. You can say it: 'Verona'." DeMond would just be like, "That's what I said: 'Vanona'."'

'Ask him about the fire in his room that he accidentally started with a maverick cigarette, the fire that got him sent to the Hole for months,' Leonard had said, with such a hearty laugh that I assumed everything worked out in the end. 'DeMond's fire will go down in the annals of Shakespeare Behind Bars' lore!'

'Ask him if he's found any weapons of mass destruction yet,' Ron Brown had suggested with a smirk.

When DeMond enters the interview room, all smiles, he is the first to admit that his last name isn't the easiest to live with, especially in this particular election year, 2004.

'Do people tease you because your last name is Bush?' I ask him.

'Yes,' DeMond laughs. 'A lot of people come up to me, "Hey, President Bush." Some people say, "Hey, President Bush. You finding weapons yet?" I hear that a lot. "You finding weapons yet?" And I know somebody playin', so I keep on walking, you know?'

But, DeMond tells me, it's rare than anyone calls him by his birth name these days. 'Most people call me Osiris, for real,' he says. 'That's my nickname. Osiris. In Greek mythology Osiris was betrayed by his brother and chopped up and then reassembled by this great love, and that's what I sort of feel like within myself, like I've been reassembled by this great love, so it's kind of a name I sort of adopted for myself.'

'In this metaphor,' I ask him, 'who's the brother that chopped you up?'

DeMond shakes his head. 'I would say just about everybody that I knew in my past. I never had a father. The first time I seen my father was in prison, and I think I was about six or seven. I had a little afro, had one of those metal picks in my fist, and I seen him, and I ran through to hug him, and the alarm went off through the door. And me and my mother were never close at all because she had four kids and she was trying to take care of those kids by herself. Me and my little brother used to stay out until, like, two o'clock, and I'm, like, nine and he's four, and we'd be out at two o'clock at night. She used to leave us with people for three or four months at a time. You know, so kind of the environment raised me. I was very emotion-less, if you can imagine that. I never was taught how to love. Drugs, sex, rock and roll. I sponged those things up. I learned it from negative influences. And if society as a whole is my brother, then my brother betrayed me.'

'Can you still hear that siren going off in your head?' I wonder.

DeMond sits up straight in his seat and shuts his eyes tight, as if the siren is going off at that very moment. 'Yes, I *always* hear that siren. When the doors close, I always hear it. The sad thing about that is my grandfather was in prison, my dad was in prison, and I'm in prison away from my son. His mother was two months pregnant when I got incarcerated, and he just turned eleven, so you know I've never been out there for him.'

'Do you think about the time when you'll get out of prison?'

'All the time,' he tells me.

'When might that happen?' I ask.

'It might happen this November,' DeMond says excitedly. 'I'm going up for parole.'

The possibility of release makes DeMond thoughtful. 'I think often about what would it be like to get out after 12 years, you know? The world is so different, and often I feel that even though I'm surrounded by eleven hundred people, that I'm alone. No one thinks alike, but even some of my closest friends, like the guys in the group, we don't view things alike.'

Specifically, the Shakespeare Behind Bars men, according to DeMond, are not as religious as he is. 'I'm a spiritual person,' DeMond says. 'It helps me to see more. For me, it's another dimension to my life, and I think without that, I would be smaller, in a sense. Right now I'm reading Martin Luther King's book. I love his book *Strength to Love*. He says, "We're in the land of misguided men and guided missiles." Walter Rauschenbusch, Dietrich Bonhoeffer, these German theologians, they're powerful guys to me. They fought for what they believed in and for equality for everyone.'

I smile. DeMond often sounds as though he's on the verge of breaking into a sermon. 'So it's not my imagination,' I say. 'When I hear you speak as Antony, and you climb up into that pulpit, I feel as though I'm transformed into maybe Reverend King's church.'

He nods. 'And that's how I look at the people I'm talking to, as my congregation.'

'You've got a seminary degree?' I ask him.

'Seminary *diploma*,' he corrects me. 'Southern Seminary, a diploma in biblical studies. I'm still thinking about getting some correspondence for my BA at Bethany College in Indiana.'

But then DeMond shifts the conversation back to our original topic of conversation. He wants to qualify what he said about having been betrayed by society, his metaphorical brother. 'I can't put the blame on the world or my brother for everything. I accept responsibility and accountability for my actions. Most of all, I'm ashamed now, if anything, you know, that I allowed myself to be led so far astray. I'm ashamed of being in here and being labeled a certain type of way because I know I'm a better human being.'

'Curt says he used to call you the "Una-Bomber" because of how you dressed when you first joined the Shakespeare program,' I tell DeMond.

He laughs. 'Oh, man. I had such a façade because my father used to . . . when he used to write to my mom every now and then and I would have a little piece of the letters before she stopped . . . before she took the letters and wouldn't let me have them anymore . . . he used to say a little bit about prison. From the way my dad described it, I thought that prison was somewhat similar to the ghetto areas I came from: wacky people all in a little bunch. So I had this façade about me, like "I don't let nobody bother me."' And when I first heard about the Shakespeare group and Curt

Tofteland, I was noticing, "Man, why this white guy come in here and dealing with us, man? What type of guy is this?" 'Cause to me – and that's another screwed up vision I had – anybody that was in the middle class was against me, but when I met Curt, I said, "Man, this guy's alright." And so I listened to him a little more. And Shakespeare is a very big piece of the puzzle to my spiritual growth.'

'You credit the Shakespeare program with having changed you?' I ask.

'Oh, yes,' DeMond answers. 'I think God used Shakespeare as the number-one tool. When you play a character, you're able to see through the character's eyes. And I was able, even when I played Tamora, to find myself saying, "If I were in that person's shoes, would I respond that way?" And it also made me think about the hurt that throughout my life I have brought other people when you look through other people's eyes. And I'm not talking about just if I got in a fight with a guy. I used to say, when I first came in, first couple of years before I got into Shakespeare, I said, "I don't wanna come back to prison. I'll never sell drugs again because I don't wanna come back to prison." But as years progressed in Shakespeare, I said, "I don't wanna sells drugs because I realize what it does to a family and what it does to a community." You know?'

'But come on,' I say, 'Wouldn't you have changed without Shakespeare?'

DeMond frowns at me. 'Yeah, but I don't know into what. One of my sayings is that the process, that is still going on with the Shakespeare, is my metamorphosis from a caterpillar to a butterfly. I'm still the same, but I'm not. I don't know if I sound girlish or what, but I feel like a butterfly. I feel like I can fly now; I'm not stuck to a certain place. I can fly. And I believe in me now. I really believe once the essence of the individual is not totally changed but starts to re-form itself, you can see it on the outside of the individual.' DeMond assumes a very low and serious voice to deliver the moral of his insect parable, but I fully believe what he's saying.

'Without Shakespeare,' he tells me 'I don't know *where* I would be. Without Shakespeare, I don't know *what* I would be.'

'What was your first role?' I ask him.

'I was a bandit in *Two Men from Verona*. And I kept saying, "Vanona". *Two Gentlemen from Vanona*. I had them laughing, these guys here. And I still have to work on my diction. Sometimes I splice New Jersey with Kentucky, and that's an awful mix. My tongue'll move fast and then it'll just slow down, you know?' Demond rolls his fists around each other in circles to illustrate just how much of a train wreck it can be. 'I really become tongue-tied.'

'Well, you can't do that with Mark Antony,' I say. 'His language has so many rhetorical flourishes.'

'And I like that because I can sit down on the words.' Yes, I think to myself, that's exactly what DeMond does. I ask him how he ever got from 'Vanona' to 'Lend me your ears.'

'I worked really hard!' he exclaims. 'And I said, "I wanna try and make it better. Try to improve myself and everything around me." Since *Two Gents* I've played Tamora and Iago and now Mark Antony, lots of great parts. Probably the best thing about being in Shakespeare is being someone else. When I'm acting, I'm not me and I'm not in prison and I'm not, you know, living with what I live with. I'm somebody else, and so I live what they live.'

I had noticed DeMond's total immersion in the role of Antony from the very first day. 'There was a moment during the final dress rehearsal when Curt was giving a note to someone whose real name is Anthony, and you responded,' I tell him.

DeMond laughs. 'Did I? Yeah, that makes sense that I would do that. I try to embody Antony. At times when I'm performing, I can feel him. It's like I really enjoy the experience. When we're doing a play, the script is like a bible to me.'

I smile. Did Mark Antony just slip another religious reference into our conversation?

'Do any of the guys ever think the Shakespeare program is too churchy or too Sunday school?' I ask.

'No, no!' DeMond says. 'The guys really love the journey for real. I would venture to say that most inmates are illiterate when they come in, and we were illiterate when we came in. We didn't know much about anything in life. And the group that is in Shakespeare is a hungry group about life. And so when they come in and see Curt, there's this big, tall man. I sort of model him like: you in this ocean and it's dark, and there's this beacon out there . . . a light. And that's Curt. And that's what prison for the most part, outside of Shakespeare, that's what prison is like. I hate to be vulgar, but a guy got raped yesterday. And it snaps you back. It's like when we leave from Shakespeare and go back to the yard, it's such a drastic difference. It's like, okay, you're back to reality.'

DeMond tells me that he feels his calling is to work with inner-city children when he is released.

'I like the story when Jesus heals the guy in the tomb, he gives him a new identity, a new name. That's somewhat like what this program with Shakespeare has done for me: a whole new identity, a whole new name. And the healed dude says, "Jesus, you changed me. Let me go with you." Jesus says, "No, you go back home. And you tell them what I've done, and you show them this light that you have become." I think it would be good for me to go to urban areas and talk to children. I know when I was a child I used to think there was street credibility for going to prison and coming out. I remember I was 15 years old, sitting on this porch with these guys, and we was smokin' a joint. And this guy pulled up in this Benz and he had a jheri curl, and all the little girls were running up, and I knew he'd just got out of prison . . . And I said, "When I get out of prison I'm gonna be just like that." At 15. Once you go to prison, you're a ghetto celebrity, and that was my highest goal at the time. And I think when I started to achieve a little of that notoriety, I didn't want to let that go because it was the only achievement I'd ever really had. But actually my heart was yearning for something bigger than that. I used to feel bad when I'd see the kids with the snotty noses and the mother giving me their food in exchange for drugs and something in me was saying, "This is not right."'

'So you want to go back to inner cities and help children to develop their problem-solving skills and critical-thinking ability so that they can think ahead to the consequences of their actions?' I ask.

DeMond's eyes get big with excitement just thinking about it. 'Exactly. In the outreach program that I founded with Sammie and Big G, when we go to the schools to speak, that's the main thing I tell the kids is that there's consequences to our actions. In that moment you're angry; or in that moment you want to smoke that joint; or in that moment you wanna drink, you just think. Just stop right there in that moment and think. I never heard anyone in my family say, "Look, I believe in you" or "I know you can do this." My mother wasn't huggy and kissy. It was more like, "I put food on your table and clothes on your back" – because that's how she was raised. So *now* I understand that. She had me at 15, and my grandmother kicked her out of the house because it was another mouth to feed. I understand that *now*; I didn't *then*. I was like, "Man, this woman hates me." I used to ask, "Am I adopted? Did you adopt me?" I was 13 when we moved to Kentucky, and at 14 I was back out on the streets, then at 15 she kicked me out. I got incarcerated at 18, and I'll be 30 in December.'

'But coming up for parole,' I remind him.

'But coming up for parole,' he replies, and he flashes me a grin that could charm the birds right out of the trees. That is, if there were any trees in sight. This is, after all, a prison. And for now it's where DeMond lives. He hasn't made parole just yet.

'Have Not You Love Enough to Bear with Me?': Ron Brown, Cassius

Of the three stars in the Shakespeare Behind Bars production of *Julius Caesar*, Ron Brown, initially at least, makes the least amount of sense to me. Ron is Cassius, my favorite character in Shakespeare's play. I like Cassius for several reasons. I like him for being a scholar. I like him for having the sense to anticipate Mark Antony's success in the forum. I like him because he shows compassion when Portia dies. I like him for having a lean and hungry look; it seems like a cool look to have. But before I watched the prison production of *Julius Caesar*, I had never thought of Cassius as *the* villain of the play. Structurally, he might be the antagonist, especially in the scenes with Brutus, but to name Cassius as the villain in a play full of murderers seems a bit reductive to me. Ron Brown plays Cassius as if he is *the* villain – angry, violent, yelling, inclined to dramatic, emotional out-bursts. This is not my idea of Cassius. During the first performance, the one in the chapel, I write in my notebook, 'Why is he so angry all the time?' And then I meet with Ron Brown.

When he walks into the interview room, Ron himself seems angry, like he'd rather not talk to me. I apologize for taking him away from his work duties in the computer lab. 'I wasn't doing any-thing important,' he says. 'Just typing in information.' When I pull out my mini tape recorders – two of them just in case one breaks and I need a backup – Ron winces. He doesn't like to be taped. He especially hates being forced to see himself on video when the Shakespeare Behind Bars members watch recordings of their per-formances. Now *this* I can relate to. It's because I'm a Virgo. I read it in Linda Goodman's *Sun Signs* book when I was a teenager, and I still remember the exact quote to this day. 'Virgos are very critical of their own photographs and fussy in the extreme about how they look, both on film and in person.'

I ask Ron, 'Are you a Virgo?'

He looks at me in shock and then makes a scoffing noise, 'Yeah.'

'I'm a Virgo, too,' I tell him. 'So I know where you're coming from. I don't ever like to see myself on video either.'

'Yeah,' Ron says.

And then I check myself. Did I just ask a convicted felon, in effect, 'What's your sign?' I don't want to give the impression that I meant it as, you know, a pick-up line.

'Are you really a Virgo?' I ask. It's not like I go around guessing peoples' astrological signs on a daily basis.

'Yeah. Are *you* really a Virgo?' Ron smirks.

'September 10th,' I say.

'September 20th,' Ron replies.

'Great,' I tell him, 'Let's get started.'

And then Ron smiles. And I realize that it's the first time I've seen him smile since I met him two days ago.

'So you play Cassius . . .' I begin.

'Yes ma'am,' Ron replies, leaning forward.

'Cassius is my favorite character in the play. But I get the feeling that you don't . . .' I stop myself short. And then I decide to just go ahead and ask him, 'Do you even like Cassius, Ron?'

Ron thinks for a moment. 'I haven't really decided whether I like him or not. I think he's not necessarily a bad person. I actually think he's good at his core. I think he's an individual who has been hurt a lot, and so he has a lot of different walls that he puts up and different façades that he portrays. I think he's very difficult to be around for long periods of time. What I did in talking to Curt was I tried to imagine what Cassius's life was prior to the beginning of the play. I think that Cassius has trouble trusting people. He's probably been involved in relationships and he's probably been hurt extremely bad and I think he's scared of being hurt again and I think the only thing that he can really put his trust in is what he can make happen for himself.'

I sit and listen, nodding politely, but Ron's interpretation of Cassius seems totally off-base to me. Cassius is suffering from a series of bad breakups? Cassius has trust issues?

'Well, what's he hurting about, in your opinion?' I ask Ron. 'I mean, Cassius tells stories about what happened in his past. Is he pissed off that he saved Caesar's life and he hasn't been rewarded for that? Is that why you think he's so angry?'

'I think anger is just the easiest emotion for people to show,' Ron says.

I look at him with utter confusion. And then I realize: Ron isn't talking about Cassius. Ron is talking about himself. It's not Cassius Ron doesn't know whether he likes or not; it's himself.

Ron continues. 'Cassius and I personally are so similar, and I didn't realize that at the beginning when I took the role. I just I knew that it was the first time I would be playing a villain.' I think to myself, there he goes again, calling Cassius a villain. But in the context of the Shakespeare Behind Bars mission, Ron's inclination to label Cassius a villain makes sense. In the Shakespeare program, volunteering to play the role of the antagonist, especially when it's an antagonist who commits a criminal act, signifies that you've reached a milestone and you're ready to deal with your past, you're ready to take accountability for your own criminal acts. Most of the men in the Shakespeare program tell me that they would rather play a woman than play 'the villain.'

I must still be frowning in confusion because Ron shifts gears. His voice lowers and his eyes soften, like he's getting ready to tell me a secret. 'You know he's intuitive, Cassius is. When he sees Caesar speaking, it's almost like watching George Bush talking on TV. He gives you all this rhetoric and all this and that and you wonder how people can believe some of the stuff he's saying.'

I giggle. Ron likes this.

'You wonder how people can believe some of the stuff Bush says, you know?' he asks me again with a raised eyebrow and his characteristic smirk.

I nod my head. I do wonder that. Often. But I never thought that I'd be having this conversation with an inmate.

'Do you think of George Bush when you're up there onstage?' I ask, surprised.

'There's a lot of people that I think of,' Ron replies. 'I mean, when you think of Julius Caesar, George Bush is like the first thing you think of. And you think of Rome and the United States and the parallels there. I mean, Rome thinks that they're the only thing that really exists. The only thing that really matters. The United States is like that also. They rule things on fear. Even the fact that we're in the war you know, you know, it's based on fear. If you asked a lot people when the war started: "Well, why are we attacking Iraq?" they would have said, "Well, because of 9/11". But I'm saying, Iraq is not specifically the ones who did that. "They may have funded Osama bin Laden." But okay, by that same token if that's the case if we're going to attack Iraq because they fund terrorism, we funded Iraq, so then we're just as guilty. Consider from the mid-1950s up until now, outside of Russia and Castro in Cuba, every single nemesis that the United States has had as a world leader has been put in place by the United States, you know, and it's like, okay, we put them there and now we finished using you for whatever it is we were using you for so now you become our enemy.'

'So when you read a Shakespeare play, you're thinking about current events?' I ask.

'Yes,' he says. 'I *prefer* to think about current events. I've been in the Shakespeare program for nine years, I'm one of the founding members, but I don't really so much have a love for Shakespeare. I have a love for *learning*. I read books. I read history. I read social sciences. I like reading philosophy, and I read some religious books, mainly comparative study.'

'Who is your favorite philosopher?' I quiz him, expecting him to cite some obscure, minor contemporary philosopher I've never read.

Without skipping a beat, Ron answers, 'René Descartes.'

'Descartes?' I ask. 'The seventeenth-century French philosopher?'

'Yeah,' Ron says. 'Mainly I fell in love with him for . . . he had a writing called *Rules for the Direction of the Mind*, and that has always stuck with me because it's like basically the limits and capabilities of any human being is only based upon the input that he puts into himself. And I agree with that. It's like, I always try to figure out why people do what they do. Why is it that we got eleven- to twelve-hundred individuals on this prison yard and we all come from different backgrounds? It can't just be "Well, your environment leads you to prison" because if that was the case everybody here would come from a disadvantageous environment and vice versa. So it's got to be something more than that.'

He just said that he 'fell in love' with Descartes, I think to myself. Who in the world falls in love with Descartes?

Ron shrugs his shoulders, 'Sometimes I over-analyze things.'

'Me too,' I tell him. 'So the Shakespeare program,' I say, 'it ain't about Shakespeare for you. Maybe it's about . . . Curt Tofteland?'

Ron nods his head. Finally I'm starting to understand him.

'Curt Tofteland is my number-one reason. He's in the top three of the most influential people in my life. I've had conversations with Curt that I guess boys probably have with their fathers. My father was never around. Last time I seen him was when I was 13. My father's a real bitter individual. He's angry. He's racist. He's mad at the world. So Curt Tofteland has become a father figure to me. He's the patriarch of Shakespeare Behind Bars.'

'Who are the other influential people in your life?' I ask.

'My grandfather and my mother.'

'Wow. So Curt's family to you.'

'Yeah, I mean there's nothing I wouldn't do for him. Me and my mother we don't really speak much now, which a lot of that is my fault. My mother she did everything she could, but I didn't understand that when I was younger. The thing about it is I don't think that she realizes how hurtful some of the things that happened were. And my grandfather . . . my father wasn't around when I grew up, so my grandfather was the closest thing that I knew to a father. He's the man in the family that everybody knows they can count on. I've never really been somebody that people can count on. I've never been anybody that *I* can really count on.'

This, I'm coming to realize, is Ron Brown's version of telling the truth about himself: focusing on his worse characteristics and nothing else. I decide to change the subject and ask him to tell me about his past Shakespeare roles.

Ron smiles. 'First Shakespeare role I ever had was Romeo. We did scenes from Shakespeare, and I was Romeo.'

'Who was Juliet?' I ask him. This oughta be good.

'I didn't do any scenes with Juliet,' he laughs. 'Thank God I avoided *that*. Which, I mean, I kinda had to go through that a little bit last year when I played Ferdinand opposite Miranda. So I've played Ferdinand, Romeo, Cassius, Malvolio, Valentine. And Emilia. I played Emilia.'

'You played Emilia in *Othello*?'

'Yeah,' Ron says, and he makes his scoffing noise again.

'Did you want to play that role?' I ask.

'No, not really,' Ron says. 'But I knew I was gonna have to get a female role.'

'Did you like anything about Emilia?'

He thinks for a while. 'I like the fact that she had integrity. At the end of the play, she didn't not face the truth even though the person that was committing the atrocities as far as orchestrating everything was her husband. But Desdemona to me is the character with the most integrity in all of Shakespeare. I mean even when she was dying and she was, like, blaming herself for it.'

The hair on the back of my neck stands on end. 'That's interesting that you target that particular moment as the height of Desdemona's integrity,' I comment. 'It's not honest at all for her to blame herself for her death. She's lying. In what way is that the height of integrity, her not naming Othello as her murderer?'

Ron explains. 'The integrity was in the fact that she loved somebody so much that even in the bleakest moment she was able to see the best in him.' I shake my head. Sounds like a romantization of spousal abuse to me. Ron continues, 'Now, I don't justify Othello because Othello was dead wrong, and I hate Othello's character.'

Ron looks up at the ceiling as if he's replaying the strangulation scene in his mind. 'It was a hard scene to watch because out of all the things I've done I've never committed a crime against a woman. So – and I guess 'cause of my sisters and my mother; I grew up with them – so it was hard 'cause I had to come on in that one scene, and Sammie had trouble with that scene, and just watching it, my heart was beating so fast, and I'm knowing intellectually that this is only a play, but it was just so difficult to watch it. It reminds me of a movie, *Looking for Mr Goodbar*. I don't know if you've ever seen that, but at the end there's a strobe light going and there's a man stabbing a woman, and the rhythm and the cinematography and everything makes it . . . it's already a horrible act, but at the same time it makes it seem more horrific. Not only are you committing this act, but it's staged and it's orchestrated and it's choreographed, and it's like, you can't even argue heat of passion.'

Ron's response to Sammie's 'Othello breakthrough' is remarkably different from any of the other inmates. He seems, interestingly enough, to think that role-playing a murder scene is actually worse than committing a real murder as a crime of passion because role-playing involves a conscious decision. Or, at least, Ron feels that it's worse for him as an audience member. Ron didn't see Sammie, one of his best friends, strangle Carol. But he did see Sammie strangle Desdemona. Rehearsal after rehearsal, performance after performance, Ron was witness to Sammie's worst side, a side that of Sammie that Ron presumably would rather forget.

I ask Ron why he thinks that Curt has the inmates perform the most violent Shakespeare plays. In nine years, Shakespeare Behind Bars has only done two comedies. 'Do you think that it's therapeutic to act in these violent plays?' I wonder. 'Do you think it was therapeutic for Sammie to play Othello?'

'Good question,' Ron says. 'I can't really speak for Sammie in response to that. I can only speak for myself. It is therapeutic for me to play Cassius, mainly from a perspective of reflectiveness and being able to have an out-of-body experience. But it's not something that I could sustain for a long period. I don't think it's good to do it year in and year out. If you do that, in order to find the characters you have to delve into an aspect of yourself that it takes you a lot of time to come to grips with. If you do it all the time, the ability to shock yourself and force yourself to look at the situation becomes just an artistic thing. You have to have some variety. And I think that you should show the comedic side and the romantic side of your personality as well; in a lot of ways, that's just as therapeutic as reenacting violent scenes. But they shy away from love stories here. A lot of people are uncomfortable with playing lovers. We've never done all of *Romeo and Juliet*. We've only done scenes. People relate to violence, but I think Curt's take on it is taking the violence and getting people to understand that it's not just about the violence; there's more to it than just the violent aspect. I understand Curt's perspective, but at the same time I don't think everybody's able to look at it that way. I don't think everybody's as in tune or insightful about the plays or the direction that Curt's trying to take the group.'

'I have to ask you a point-blank question,' I warn Ron.

Ron scowls. 'Most questions *should* be point-blank.'

'All right,' I admit, 'that's my way of trying to be polite. What I'm saying is if you don't want to tell me the answer to this you don't have to.'

'Go ahead,' he says. 'I'm an open book.'

And so I ask him. 'Why do you have such a stiff sentence for your kidnapping conviction?' Life without parole for 25 years.

Ron pauses. And then says, slowly, quietly and sadly, 'Because my hostage was not released alive.'

I say nothing. The room is silent. I can hear the whirring of the fan behind me.

'That's about as point-blank an answer as you can get. That is the reason why Cassius and I are related to each other.' Ron continues, 'I was in a situation where basically . . .' his voice trails off. He tries again. 'It didn't really seem real at the time. At the time, I didn't remember a whole lot of things, but at the end of the day, I kidnapped somebody and shot this person for no reason. And I affected somebody's life. Not just his, but his family's and my family's. And I've been fortunate in the respect that I could've gotten the death penalty but I didn't. The state of West Virginia has seen fit not to try me for murder. I was 19 years old and had no clue about anything. I was trying to be something that I wasn't.'

'Was anybody else involved?' I ask.

'No, just me,' Ron replies. 'I wasn't drunk. I wasn't high or anything like that. I was just emotionally and psychologically overloaded. I regret it, and I hate the fact that I took somebody's life for no reason.'

Ron shifts in his chair. He's angry again. He's angry with himself. He's been angry with himself for a while.

'It would almost be easier if I could say this person did something to me. Still, though, the end doesn't justify the means. I had tried to commit suicide once before I got incarcerated, and inside I was just empty, completely empty. And I went from trying to destroy myself, and not really wanting to destroy myself but not knowing how to ask for help, to turning it outwards on someone else. And I wish that I had never done that. And I think a lot of times I would rather have been successful at suicide than successful at murder, you know? I think about it a lot. And it makes it difficult for me when people say stuff about my performances in the Shakespeare plays. When the people in the audience say: "You did a good job," it's like, "So what? I just did a play. That's all it was. You don't even know me. You don't know if I'm a good person or not. This one thing, being in a Shakespeare play, this one thing will absolve me of something?"'

'Is it hard to forgive yourself for what happened?' I ask.

Ron thinks for a long time. 'I don't know if the word is "hard" or "impossible" or somewhere in between,' he say. 'I'm going to have a re-sentencing hearing soon, and I expressed to the lawyer and the judge, regardless of whether or not you lessen my time, I would like to speak to the family and just express that I'm really sorry about the situation. I know that doesn't mean nothing. But they don't even really know what happened. And I want them to know that I didn't plan it, I didn't plan to kill him, and it wasn't like he suffered or anything, and I know it doesn't take away their loss, but, I don't know, maybe I could offer some closure or whatever to the situation.'

I don't reply. I just listen. Ron continues, 'The reality is that no matter what happened to me when I was younger, no matter what my mother said to me, no matter whether my father was there or not there, there's still a responsibility that I have to make decisions. I had a time in my life where I didn't make no decisions. I was 19 years old. And I thought I was a man at the time, but I had no clue what manhood was about. I had no clue what being responsible for my actions and taking responsibility for them was. Consequently, somebody got hurt. Maybe the world says that I don't deserve to be out. If it's a situation about only punishment, I guess that may be the case. If it's about repaying a debt to society and trying to turn the situation into something positive for other people, maybe I will get out. It kind of comes down to what other people think. But I had to decide within myself what I was going to be. Whether I was going to be that type of person. Regardless of what happened, you have to make a decision. Do you want to live or do you want to just slowly die?'

Over the course of the rest of the week, Ron Brown becomes my favorite person to converse with. We talk about Emerson and Thoreau. We talk about Malcolm X and Muhammad Ali. We talk about his favorite movies – he's a romantic comedy fan, *Jerry Maguire*, that sort of thing. Ron is smart and quick. When I jokingly blame my astrological sign for my shortcomings, Ron replies, 'Didn't you read the play, Professor? The fault is not in your stars, but in yourself.' After the final performance of *Julius Caesar*, the cast members circulate their programs for visitors to sign. This is an annual tradition, but Ron's too cool to have done it in the past, so I'm surprised when he approaches me with program and pen in hand. 'This is the first time I ever asked anyone to sign a program,' he says. 'This is the inaugural signing,' he repeats as I'm writing. 'Yeah, I heard ya,' I say to him as I hand back his program. Ron looks at my inscription and smiles. 'What did she write, man?' Shane asks. Ron shakes his head and laughs. 'She wrote, "You had me at Descartes."'

Intermission

Othello Unplugged at the Luther Luckett Correctional Complex

When I reunite with Ron, DeMond, Sammie and the other SBB actors, two months have passed. Tofteland's professional company, the Kentucky Shakespeare Festival, is in full swing, and they have brought their production of Othello to Luckett for one performance. Phill Cherry plays the title role. I had met Phill at the performance of *Julius Caesar* in the Visitor's Room. A longtime supporter of SBB, and a personal friend to many of the men, especially Sammie and DeMond, Phill saw the SBB *Othello* production back in 1999 and witnessed Sammie's emotionally moving performance. More importantly, Phill knows just how difficult it is for Sammie to watch any production of this particular play. Nevertheless, Sammie is the first to arrive at the performance, seating himself very purposefully and deliberately in the center of the front row. At the end of the first half when Curt announces that the actors will take a short break, I see Phill wink at Sammie as if to ask, 'How you holding up?'

But other than that secret message between friends, Sammie doesn't receive any special attention from anyone. When I circulate during intermission, it seems to be business as usual with these guys. Ron tells me that he finds Iago reminiscent of President Bush; Shane tries to chat up the actress playing Bianca; Big G gives me a big hug. When we return to our seats, Curt announces that there's not enough time to do the entire second half of the play; the SBB men have to report for count by noon. One KSF actor suggests that they at least do Act 5, Scene 2, but there's some confusion about how it starts. As Phill struggles to find the top of the scene, Sammie playfully says, 'Come on, Rookie.' But there's a gravity in his voice that tells me Sammie knows exactly what's coming and he isn't exactly sure how he'll react.

When Othello strangles Desdemona, I look around the room to gauge the men's reactions. DeMond covers his face with his hand. Ron closes his eyes entirely and keeps them closed for several minutes. Sammie watches the whole thing, staring straight at the murder, like he's taking his medicine. Tears stream down his face, but his posture is upright, never flinching.

Because the KSF actors limited the second half of their performance, there's enough time for Curt to lead a question and answer session. DeMond raises his hand.

'With Othello and Desdemona,' he says, 'the interaction, it was a beautiful picture, just to see how he's really passionate and tender with her. This was someone in his life that he really cared about, and theirs was a beautiful love. And what's messing me up is him killing her. Because just an hour ago, he was like, "This is my beauty. This is everything in the world to me. And I love her so much." And then he's choking her to death, you know?'

Curt responds. 'DeMond, I think that last description that you gave is what for me is at the heart of this play. He's choking her and thinking, "You deserve to die for what you did to me." But Desdemona's infidelity isn't true. She didn't cheat on him.'

Sammie says, 'Yeah.'

Curt continues. 'But even if it were true, even if she did cheat on him, is that a reason for her to die?'

DeMond doesn't answer. DeMond played Iago in the 1999 production. Since then, he's been writing a prequel to Shakespeare's play based upon Othello's early days. DeMond knows full well how Shakespeare's play ends. But he seemed to be hoping, along with so many of us who are rooting for the newlyweds from the beginning of the play, that Othello was going to wise up this time and that he and Desdemona were going to live happily ever after. 'She made him a better human being just because he had this love in his life that he had never had before, so she made him better, and he was choking her. And it's just . . . I don't know. What he did to her, man, it's just messed up.'

Curt says, 'There are three powerful lines in this play. Desdemona says, "I saw Othello's visage in his mind." And Othello says, "She gave me a world of kisses." And right at the end, "I kissed thee ere I killed thee."'

But Sammie has found another line that deserves mention. Sammie speaks, and unlike DeMond he doesn't raise his hand. 'I heard Othello say at the very end: "But why should honor outlive honesty? Let it go."'

'He's blowing it to heaven,' Curt responds. 'Othello is saying, "It is too late." But when is it ever too late?'

'Never,' Sammie says, without missing a beat.

'It is *never* too late.'

That evening I attend the KSF performance of *Othello* in the Louisville, city park with my buddy Karen Heath and her girlfriend. As the longtime staff liaison for SBB, Karen has supervised all of the rehearsals and performances for years, including the *Othello* rehearsals back in 1999. Though she's told me her *Othello* story at least three times, I never tire of hearing it. 'I'll always remember that day in the Visitor's Room when Sammie had his breakdown,' Karen says. 'He finished the scene. And he was sobbing. He was just *sobbing*. Curt said, "Good. Again." And I thought to myself, "Is Curt crazy? Has he totally lost his mind? These guys are going to kill him."' Then Karen tells me about Mike Smith's portrayal of Desdemona. 'Sammie cried during the strangling scene, and anyone who came to a rehearsal or a performance could see that Sammie was crying,' she says. 'But what you couldn't see was that during the whole scene Mike was crying too.'

During intermission at the Shakespeare in the Park performance of *Othello*, Karen asks me how I like the show so far. I tell her that watching the KSF actors in the park is not one ounce as powerful as watching the performance as Luckett that afternoon. And, even more than that, the professional *Othello* isn't anywhere close to being as good as the prison *Julius Caesar*. The professional actors just aren't as good as the Shakespeare Behind Bars actors. Karen agrees. 'Well,' she says, 'you know the reason for that. The Shakespeare in the Park actors do Shakespeare in order to make a living. The Shakespeare Behind Bars actors do Shakespeare in order to live.'

Act 3

The Luckett Symposium on Race and Shakespeare: *Titus Andronicus, Merchant of Venice,* and *Othello*

When it comes to casting their shows, prison theatre companies are downright revolutionary in that the actor's ethnicity and gender – the two demographic categories that probably matter the most to professional casting agents – simply cannot factor into casting decisions in prison productions in the way that they do in other venues. Programs like Shakespeare Behind Bars and Prison Performing Arts rehearse for five to nine months per show. At any point during the process, one of the inmates may be shipped to another prison, sent to solitary or decide to quit. Normally, the directors lose up to 10 actors per production. When this happens, the parts rotate at the last minute, sometimes just weeks before the show goes up, the actor's ethnicity is the farthest thing from anyone's mind.

But more than just a matter of necessity and practically, Shakespeare Behind Bars' color-blind policy when it comes to casting is a result of Tofteland's insistence that the inmates choose roles that will force them to deal with their pasts. The most important factor in the self-casting process is that the inmate identifies with or is tested by the Shakespearean character in some way. DeMond, for instance, chose the role of Tamora, nevermind that he's a black man and she's a Scandinavian woman because, like Tamora, two of his children have died. Similarly, he took the role of Iago for the challenge of it. He liked Iago because 'he was a little crazy' and 'took him for a loop.' Who cares if Iago is 'a tricky white dude'? For decades, the RSC has claimed to employ a color-blind casting policy; prison theatre companies like Shakespeare Behind Bars actually do it.

One of the unhappy causes of the diversity in prison theatre productions is the fact that there is a significantly disproportionate number of black men incarcerated in the US. Though African-American men make up only six percent of the US population, more than half of the men in prison are African-American, and in several states, like Illinois and Michigan, black men comprise almost 70 percent of the male inmate population. According to the Bureau of Justice, in 2004, there are 3,218 black men in prison per 100,000 black men in the US, compared to 463 white men per 100,000. I would venture to say that many of the best black Shakespearean actors in America are behind bars.

When it comes to Shakespeare Behind Bars, the actors' ethnicities and life experiences provide possibilities for radical, enlightening interpretations of Shakespeare. The very style of memorizing lines is inspired by the call-and-response format of black institutions, and the inmates' role models when it comes to their delivery of Shakespeare's verse aren't Laurence Olivier and John Gielgud; they're Martin Luther King and Malcolm X.

Sometimes, Marcel Herriford tells me, there's a little Hollywood mixed in for good measure. 'DeMond thinks he's the next Denzel Washington, for real,' Marcel laughs, 'I tell him, "You're not there yet."' But playing the role of the Soothsayer gives Marcel plenty of time to listen to DeMond's performance of Mark Antony, and that performance definitely puts Marcel in mind of someone. 'What excites me about seeing Mark Antony do his speech,' Marcel tells me, 'is that I look at him as Malcolm X. I like Malcolm more than anyone. Not taking nothing away from Martin, but Malcolm is sort of like an idol to me. So when DeMond plays Mark Antony, and when he makes his gestures and the way tears come down his face, when I am sitting there, I see Malcolm. And the words make my heart flutter.'

However, other than the passing reference, like DeMond confessing that he was initially skeptical of Curt because he's a 'white guy,' the Shakespeare Behind Bars members hardly ever mention race. They don't talk about race when it comes to their own group dynamics, and they also don't talk about race in Shakespeare's plays. One inmate tells me, off the record, that no one dares broach the topic because 'it's not politically correct.'

One exception to this rule is Ron Brown, who 'took a break' from the Shakespeare program in 2001, the year that the group produced *Titus Andronicus*. '*Titus Andronicus* was too much for me,' Ron says. 'I didn't like the fact that the Moor, Aaron, is portrayed and written as an unrepentant, evil individual. He doesn't care. Even at the end, just right at the end, he says, "I'll knock on people's doors, and dig the bodies of their loved ones up and leave them on their steps somewhere." And then you have what happens to Lavinia, of course. The whole thing I just didn't like.' From 1999 when the group performed *Othello*, Ron found himself upset with Shakespeare's representation of black men. 'I *hate* Othello's character,' Ron tells me. 'I *hate* his character. Othello is representative of individuals with so much potential that allow themselves to be led in a way that's destructive to them. He represents every individual that gets talked into gangs, every individual that listens to rap songs and thinks it's all right to put your hands on women and never take responsibility for that.'

The Shakespeare Behind Bars approach to racial conflict and racial slurs in the plays seems to be not to talk about them directly. And on at least one occasion the group has edited racism out of Shakespeare. As part of an evening of scenes from Shakespeare, Shane Williams performed the monologue from *Two Gentlemen of Verona* in which Proteus tries to decide whether to stick with his girlfriend Julia or pursue his best friend's beloved, Silvia. Proteus says that 'Silvia – witness Heaven, that made her fair! | Shows Julia but a swarthy Ethiope'. When Williams performed the scene, he changed the word 'Ethiope' to 'witch.' After the show, I asked Shane if he had altered the original line on purpose, in an attempt to make the text more respectful of African women. Shane said, 'I didn't do anything. That's all Curt. I never even read the whole play. Curt just gave me the scene and said, "Memorize this."' For Tofteland, who prides himself on leading the only men's prison company that produces the plays exactly as they appear in the First Folio, to have altered the text is significant.

Later Sammie tells me, 'When it comes to blacks and whites, Shakespeare Behind Bars is a unique group in the sense that we don't see.' Though Sammie takes the party line, other Shakespeare Behind Bars members qualify his statement.

'The issue of race is *there*,' DeMond tells me, 'but it's not a *big* issue for us.'

'It's an *unspoken* issue,' Ron says, and DeMond agrees, 'Yeah, it's an *unspoken* issue.' And so, at the end of July 2004, I head back to Luckett where I meet with Sammie, DeMond, and Ron, and ask them if there's anything they want to say.

When we sit down as a group, the men are reluctant to talk. 'It's not about race; it's about humanity,' DeMond tells me. 'If anything, class is a bigger issue than race.'

'We don't think of it in terms of race when we're casting or anything,' Sammie insists.

Ron interjects. 'I think about it, you know what I'm saying? But at the same time, it's kind of counterproductive to have thoughts about certain things. We have people that come and go. Some people black; some people white. Whatever.'

'I understand that when it comes to casting race isn't an issue,' I reply, 'but within some of Shakespeare's plays race is definitely an issue. Paul Robeson always said that *Othello* is a play about racial conflict. Do you disagree with Robeson?'

Sammie immediately answers, 'I actually do agree with Robeson. If you look at Iago and his reasoning for his total disgust of the Moor it's quite clear . . .'

DeMond interupts. 'Because Iago says, "Not to affect many proposed matches of your own clime and complexion," and "When she seemed to shake and fear your looks she loved you most." So he talks about his color and basically he paints black as bad and then Othello turns . . .'

'. . . And then,' Sammie interjects, taking the floor back, 'Othello says, "For I am black and have not those soft parts of conversation that chamberers have."'

'Yeah,' DeMond says. 'And then Othello gets angry. He says, "Oh, black vengeance!"'

'So Shakespeare portrays black as bad in that sense,' Sammie concludes.

DeMond goes one step further. 'Yeah. Normally, Moors are painted as either warriors or vicious or animals or aggressive.'

'In Shakespeare?' I ask him.

'In Shakespeare,' DeMond says. 'Moors are vicious and animalistic and aggressive and warriors. I think, to my knowledge, Othello is the only one who shows some compassion and makes it to real high ranks and is respected. And that's another thing about Iago. Iago disliked Othello to be in his position: "You a Moor, and you not supposed to be in that position. *I'm* supposed to be in that position."'

And then Ron weighs in. 'I think Shakespeare is *lacking* in his knowledge of black men. Now regardless of what the reason behind that was – if he wasn't exposed to them or what – his view of black men is small or skewed. What I took from *Othello* was the message that all you've got to do is dig at black man, dig at a black man, and you'll get him to self-destruct.'

Ron continues, 'But even more so in *Titus Andronicus* with the material of Aaron and Tamora. You've got Tamora; she's twisted herself. But Aaron, no matter how twisted Tamora may be . . .'

DeMond nods his head enthusiastically, 'Yeah, Aaron's a supervillain.'

'Yeah,' Ron says, 'She's got some type of maternal something – I don't know if you call it instincts, but she's got something. But Aaron is a sick, twisted puppy . . .'

'Yeah,' Sammie agrees.

Ron keeps going. 'And Aaron is bereft of any redeemable quality . . .'

'And he could be anyone, black or white,' Sammie says triumphantly.

Ron looks at Sammie. 'But the point is . . .'

'He's not,' I say.

'He's not,' Demond agrees.

'He's not,' Ron says. 'And I think about that. I have not, to this day, seen any black Shakespearean character – and I haven't read all the Shakespeare plays; I haven't even read half of them – but I've not seen a black person that has a certain level of integrity or honesty about him to where he is able to be strong and is not manipulated or anything like that.'

DeMond comes to Shakespeare's defense. 'In *Merchant of Venice*, Portia talks about the dark-skinned guy, the Prince of Morocco, and she finds him very beautiful in looking upon him. That was interesting to me when I read that six years ago.'

Sammie remembers an even more compelling passage. 'In *Two Gentlemen of Verona*, Shakespeare made the statement, "Black men are beauteous pearls in ladies eyes."' The line is actually 'Black men are pearls in beauteous ladies eyes,' but there's no chance to get a word in edgeway.

'Aggressiveness, sexual prowess . . .' Ron continues, raising his hand as he counts off the attributes on his fingers.

Sammie is defiant. 'No, *beautiful*.'

DeMond asks for a point of clarification. 'Now do you mean beautiful as in, you know, "Man, he could tear me up?"'

Ron shakes his head. 'But all those things are tied in. There's some white people I know who haven't been associated with a lot of black individuals, but the projection that they will have by looking at television or whatever would be, okay black men are really aggressive. They talk about . . . just the myths that go on about us and there's just a curiosity about us but they don't really know us, you know what I'm saying? There's no understanding of the deeper qualities that go past the physical in any way, whether it's who we are as individuals, the integrity we might have, or our ability to be responsible.'

'On the other hand,' DeMond says, 'I would have to say, personally, you know, that Shakespeare could've made just every moment or thought about someone with dark skin horrible. There could've been a time where Othello had no redemption in him at all. There could've been a time where Aaron chopped off his *baby's* head.'

'Speaking of *Titus*, what do you think about the ending?' I ask the men. 'Lucius' denunciation of Aaron is full of racial slurs. And yet, in Shakespeare's play, Titus is the one who starts the violence. What do you think Shakespeare is up to?'

'Sure, you have adults saying all that racist stuff,' Sammie says, 'but the play ends with young Lucius in charge, the next generation. So who's to say? Will he follow in the footsteps of his family or will he change?'

'You could argue that Titus's killing was honorable but Aaron is the evil killing,' DeMond suggests. 'That reminds me of how when it comes to the Civil War everybody says, "Both generals were good and honorable" even though they were both killing. But when Nat Turner went around and said, "Man, I don't wanna be your slave and you're wrong and you're gonna set us free or I'm gonna kill every farmer from plantation to plantation," he's horrible and you'd better not speak about him in anybody's history class, you know? And then on the flip side, Aaron was already an evil character, so I guess at the end of the play you always want the evil guy to get it and the good guy to win and be triumphant. In any story you've got to have the good guy and the bad guy.'

'Sammie made a valid point, though,' Ron interjects. 'As far as Aaron's concerned, there's really no history there. At least with Titus, you have some sense of who he was, so what happens is you've got an uneven playing ground to begin with. I don't know the chronology of when these plays were written in Shakespeare's life, but I'll be willing to bet that *Titus Andronicus* was written before *Othello* and *Merchant of Venice*.'

'You're right,' I tell him. '*Titus* was about 10 years before *Othello*.'

Ron nods. He figured that was the case. 'So in *Titus* you can tell that Shakespeare has no knowledge except for that blacks are probably aggressive. So he's limited. Now when he wrote *Othello*, maybe he had seen something in his life so that he could envision black men as individuals capable of remorse.'

'And being gentle,' Sammie says.

'Compassion . . . this aspect of personality that is not warlike . . .' Ron continues, counting on his fingers again. 'But when I look at Aaron . . . I hated the *Titus* play myself. It was just . . . from the fact of the raping . . .'

'The tongue cutting . . .' DeMond looks at me and shakes his head.

'And it was like Shakespeare had a real jacked-up view of the world,' Ron concludes.

'Yeah,' Sammie confesses. 'We were calling him twisted.'

'George Bush Doesn't Care about Black People': Post-Katrina *Julius Caesar* at Northeast Correctional Center

Though Agnes Wilcox began her prison work at around the same time as Tofteland, their programs grew up in relative isolation. Wilcox received national attention in 2002 when her Prison Performing Arts production of *Hamlet* at the Missouri Eastern Correctional Center near St Louis was featured by reporter Ira Glass on the National Public Radio show *This American Life*. Since institutional rules at the maximum-security prison would not allow the cast of inmates to be in the same room as their audience long enough to perform Shakespeare's play in its entirety, Wilcox's group staged *Hamlet* one act at a time over the course of three years.

Wilcox made fragmentation the theme of her production. Hamlet was played by a chorus of four men who were always on stage together and divided Hamlet's lines amongst themselves, a casting choice that underscored Hamlet's complex psyche and conflicted morality. Since 2003, Wilcox's organization has diversified to include programs at medium-security men's prisons as well as programs for incarcerated women, juvenile offenders, and at-risk youth. But no matter the security level at each venue, Wilcox's actors always perform only one or two acts of the play at a time. The second half of each prison show is devoted to the inmates' original work, and it frequently takes the form of spoken word poetry recitations and performances of original rap songs.

In January 2006, Wilcox invites me to the Northeast Correctional Center in Bowling Green, Missouri for the performance of *Julius Caesar: Acts Two and Three*. The play is performed superbly and costumed beautifully in modern-day dress with the conspirators in three-piece suits and ties and Caesar in army fatigues. Nevertheless, it is the after-show that I find the most compelling.

At first, I don't expect it to be good. The after-show begins with the actor who plays Artimedorus, Rashid Toney, incarcerated for 34 years, announcing that we're going to hear a 'Shakespeare rap.' I groan inwardly, anticipating something amateurish and silly, something similar to Reduced Shakespeare Company's rap about Othello: 'He liked white women, and he like green jello.' Oh no, I think. This is talent-show part of the evening where the inmates present their bad, rhyming couplet poetry, and even though it's crappy poetry, the audience either roars with laughter or cries, not because the poetry is any good but only because the inmates' situation itself is so full of pathos.

Five African-American men return to the stage, arrange their chairs in a half circle, and sit with their bodies leaning forward, their forearms resting on their legs, eyes down, nodding their heads to the beat, shaking their heads back and forth slowly, thoughtfully. The group includes Tim Norman, grandson of a former member of Ike and Tina Turner's band, and Lavell 'City Spud' Webb, a founding member of the St Lunatics and one of hip-hop artist Nelly's best friends. If you've heard Nelly's hit song 'Ride Wit' Me,' you've heard City. For their *Julius Caesar* after-show performance, though, the five PPA rappers are introduced by their Shakespeare names – Brutus, Cassius, Mark Antony, Decius Brutus, and Popilius – as though the Shakespeare group has provided them with a new identity.

But the rap is not about Shakespeare. It's not even about Rome. It's about America. And the tyrant isn't Julius Caesar. It's George W. Bush.

I sit listening in awe as the PPA group delivers an extensive, six-stanza rap critiquing the Bush administration, particularly for their mishandling of Hurricane Katrina. The prison rappers blame the Federal Emergency Management Agency (FEMA) for not being prepared for the national disaster. Each man calls out Bush by name several times, accusing him of 'trippin' on Iraq' and engaging in an unjustified war instead of focusing on problems at home. The rappers are especially critical of Bush's authorization of the shooting of people in New Orleans who were looting – 'Bush said: "Shoot to kill,"' the rappers announce with disdain.

As the song continues, the men express their sympathy for the victims' families, and then they explain how the tragedy of Hurricane Katrina, and the subsequent separation of families, makes them think of their own situation. In the metaphor that the rappers introduce, they are themselves in the midst of a national disaster – the disaster that is the imprisonment of generation after generation of black men – and they mourn that they are being kept apart from their loved ones. One man says that he thinks of his father in New Orleans. Another says that he misses his daughter in Chicago. After each stanza, the men join together as a chorus to sing the hook:

America
Land of the free
Look whatcha done to me.

America,
If I was drowning
Would you save me?

The 'Shakespeare rap' has two effects. First, it likens the situation of black people, especially black men, in the US to a national disaster for which the American Government and society were not only unprepared but have totally mishandled. The rappers suggest that because of their ethnicity they have not been treated as human, not been worth saving. The upshot is that the US is content to throw away black men. The 'Shakespeare rap' holds the government as least partly responsible for the disproportionate percentage of black people in prison. In its sentiment, it is reminiscent of fellow rapper Kanye West's controversial accusation on national television during the post-Katrina fundraising drive: 'George Bush doesn't care about black people.'

Secondly, the 'Shakespeare rap' functions as an epilogue to their *Julius Caesar* peformance, an epilogue that calls for a radical reinter-pretation of the production. It says, 'In this play about empire, about ambition, secret alliances, rhetoric, conspiracy, assassination, we are people who think about politics. That play you just saw us do? When we played *Julius Caesar* in modern dress, we were thinking about modern times, our time, our politicians. To us, it's not about Rome; it's about home.' Even the costume choices – conspirators dressed as congressmen in business suits, Caesar dressed in army fatigues – become more poignant after hearing the 'Shakespeare rap.'

Although the men in Prison Performing Arts might be more politically outspoken than those in Shakespeare Behind Bars, both groups are similar in their eagerness to testify to the importance of the programs to their lives. During the talkback session, Gary Riley, who plays the Soothsayer, says, 'This program has changed my life. I used to be in so much mess. Originally, I didn't even want to be in this Shakespeare play. But in the end, we worked as a team. All these brothers working with me. We came as one together.'

Alan Norwood, a plebian, agrees, 'If I hadn't got into this program, I would've gotten written up and been in the Hole.'

'Acting is such a delight,' says Antonio Graves, who plays Cassius. 'And this program is not just about acting but looking inside ourselves. The exercises we do allow everyone to be who they are; you can't cover it up. At first I was skeptical about joining the program, but everyone made me feel comfortable. A lot of guys in the yard didn't take us seriously at first. We were coming out of chow with books in our hands, talking to ourselves in our cells. But eventually they came around. The thing is, doing this you become a leader. We take that stand. We want to change for the better. We want to cause others to change for the better. We wear our PPA Shakespeare t-shirts around the yard like a badge of honor. There are no shmucks on this stage. This program changes people's lives more than I can say.'

Another significant difference between Tofteland's program and Wilcox's is that while the Shakespeare Behind Bars men perform the women's roles, the men in the PPA productions perform with professional actresses. Wilcox's choice to have the men act with women is not less progressive by any stretch of the imagination. Indeed, given any and every US prison's strict codes limiting the interactions between male inmates and female visitors, Wilcox's mixed-sex casts are one of the most remarkable things about her program. Whether male inmates play men opposite *men* who play women or male inmates play men opposite *women* who play women, it is impossible for any performance in a secure, restricted, same-sex setting *not* to be radical when it comes to gender and sexuality. However, playing a love scene opposite a 'real live woman' does alleviate a very real danger for male inmates, the increased risk of being sexually abused by other inmates on the yard. Acting with women also relieves any anxiety that the PPA inmates might feel about being lovey-dovey with their male counterparts, not to mention one quite compelling fringe benefit for any heterosexual man that comes with performing with a woman: she's a woman!

After the talkback, I ask Tim Norman, who plays Brutus, what it was like to rehearse and perform with a woman after having been locked up and segregated from women for several years. 'Initially, I was really shy about it,' he says. 'I came into the rehearsal and saw her and said, "I don't know if I can do this; she looks kinda pretty."' Tim continues. 'I thought we'd just stand on opposite sides of the stage and say our lines to each other, but during the very first rehearsal, Agnes told me, "Touch her!"'

'You could get in trouble for that?' I ask.

'Oh yeah!' Tim replies, glancing around the room at the prison staff and lowering his voice. 'Those white shirts will let us have it for just *looking* at you for too long. But everything went well. We all have fun together, and we treat the women like they are just one of the guys, you know?'

'It was nice, huh?' I smile. 'To be able to touch a woman again?'

Tim laughs and nods his head. 'Hell yeah, it was nice. Some guys were wanting to join the group just for that!'

I tell Tim about the Shakespeare Behind Bars group in Kentucky and ask if he thinks the PPA men, who are certainly as talented as the Kentucky group, could handle men playing all the roles, including the women's parts.

'No way,' he practically yells at me.

'You wouldn't be willing to play a woman?' I ask.

'No way,' Tim repeats. 'This is prison. If I went around acting like a woman, there would be serious consequences on the yard.'

But the men in Shakespeare Behind Bars have been sharing the female roles amongst themselves since the group was founded in 1995 without any incident of 'serious consequences.' On the contrary, most of the inmates at Luckett admire the Shakespeare Behind Bars actors who take on the challenge of playing women. And sometimes, like when the group tours to the nearby women's prison, the Shakespeare Behind Bars actors find that they are admired by the ladies, too.

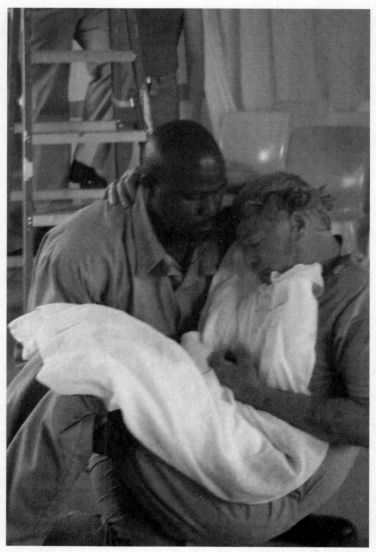

Mark Antony (DeMond Bush) cradles the body of Julius Caesar (Floyd Vaughn) in his arms as Brutus (Sammie Byron) ascends the pulpit.

Photo by Amy Scott-Douglass

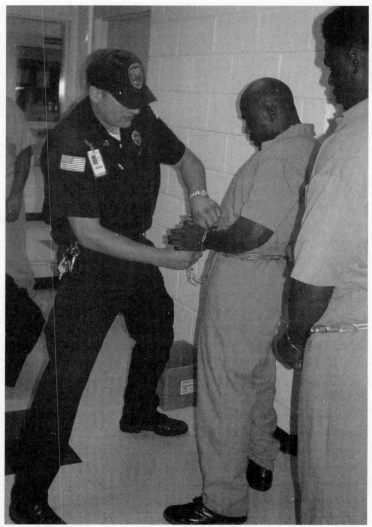

After the Julius Caesar *performance at the Kentucky Correctional Institute for Women, a prison guard chains DeMond Bush and Anthony Silver in preparation for their transport back to Luther Luckett Correctional Complex.*

Photo by Curt Tofteland

Act 4

'Romans, Countrymen, Lovers!': The SBB Tour at the Kentucky Correctional Institute for Women

Being a guest at a women's prison when a visiting men's theatre company is in residence for the afternoon is like being a chaperone at a junior high dance. On 3 September 2004, a hundred women – those who earned the highest marks in their college courses at Kentucky Correctional Institute for Women – are invited to the prison cafeteria for the Shakespeare Behind Bars's touring performance of *Julius Caesar*. And let me tell you, the KCIW women don't come for the Shakespeare; they come for the men. As the women filter into the room, their eyes search out the boys. I hear one woman say, 'Oooh, there's a nice one,' like she's picking out a lobster at a restaurant.

I take a seat in the front row, but a guard quickly approaches me. 'You can't sit there, ma'am,' he says. 'We need to seat you somewhere safe. You can't sit next to the inmates.' I stand up, obedient but disappointed. The whole point of me coming to this performance was to get to know the women. But I've been in prisons long enough to have learned that there's only one person who has the final say, and that's the warden. I walk up to the warden, introduce myself, thank her for allowing me to visit her prison, and ask if I may please sit with the inmates. 'Yes, of course!' she happily replies. I return to the prison guard and announce that I have the warden's permission to sit with the inmates. 'Oh then, by all means, ma'am,' he says politely, and he sits me in between a brunette, a blonde, and a redhead. Their names, they tell me, are Amanda, Towanda, and Zola Zee. They are beautiful, stunningly beautiful. And they're on the prowl.

The brunette, Amanda, recognizes Big G from the 2003 *Tempest* tour. 'He was in it last year,' she whispers to me. 'He's funny.' Redheaded Zola Zee takes a shine to Leonard, who, as Lucius, plays a sort of Renaissance-style version of Led Zeppelin's 'Stairway to Heaven' on his guitar. 'That was my high-school class song,' Zola Zee swoons. But Towanda, the blonde, is the most dedicated shopper of the three. Once she realizes that I actually know the men, she puts me to work. 'Who's the light-skinned one?' she asks, pointing at Shane. And then her attention shifts to Ron. 'Oh my goodness,' she exclaims, 'Who is that? He's beautiful!' The scene between Cassius, Brutus, and Casca sends Towanda into absolute bliss. She literally moans throughout it.

But she snaps out of it, at least temporarily, during the assassination scene. 'Stop that!' she insists, as the conspirators begin to attack Caesar. 'No! You can't do that!'

'That's why they're in here, dammit,' Zola Zee laughs nervously.

One woman from across the room notices that the wounded Caesar is still moving and announces to the other women, 'He's still alive!' When the conspirators go to stab Caesar again, Towanda screams, 'No!'

'Ah, yuck!' says Amanda as the men wash their hands in Caesar's blood. 'Jeez. That's totally gross.'

'There's a lot of death in this play,' Zola Zee notes.

'They're mean,' Towanda says.

'This play isn't half as good as *The Tempest*,' Amanda complains. 'Now *that* play was funny. There was a rap song in that. And the men danced for us. We liked that.'

Later, another woman across the room hears Brutus refer to the Poet as a 'jigging fool,' and cracks up laughing. I'm pretty sure she thinks he's said 'jiggy fool.' The women seem to want to make *Julius Caesar* a comedy whether it is or not. In particular, they find the scenes between Brutus and Portia, and Caesar and Calpurnia absolutely hysterical. Both of the women are performed by Hal Cobb, who has a long history of playing female roles in Shakespeare Behind Bars productions. At the Luckett performances, Cobb was praised. One professional actor in the audience told Hal, 'In all of the years that I have seen actresses do the Portia/Brutus scene, I felt like your Portia was the most invested in her relationship with Brutus.' But the prison women are having none of that. They respond to the scene in which Portia shows Brutus her self-inflicted wound as if it were a Bickersons episode or a Punch and Judy puppet show, laughing so hard that tears pour out of their eyes. The scene in which Calpurnia warns Caesar about her dream sends them into hysterics. But they don't like the offhanded sexist remarks in the play. They dislike Portia's appraisal of herself as having 'a man's mind but a woman's [little] might'; they scowl when she says, 'Ay me, how weak a thing | The heart of woman is!' Cassius' accusation that any cowardly conspirators are 'womanish' makes the KCIW inmates shake their heads in disapproval, and Brutus' comment about cowardliness and 'the melting spirits of women' receives a 'What?' look from a woman across from me.

As the first half of the play draws to an end, Towanda is still fixated on Ron. 'You go over there right now,' she instructs me, motioning to the area where the men are sitting, 'and tell Ron Brown that Towanda is in love with him for life. He's beautiful. Mmm hmm.'

The men thrive on the energy that the women direct toward them. During the talkback session, it takes only three questions before the flirting begins.

'What play are you going to do next year?'

'*Timon of Athens.*'

'How long did it take you to get this production ready?'

'Nine months.'

'What inspired you to become a member of Shakespeare Behind Bars?'

'I heard we got to come over here and see you ladies.' The women giggle and blush.

The women ask DeMond, 'Were those real tears you cried onstage?'

DeMond explains that the reason he's able to cry on cue is that he just thinks about how important his Shakespeare brothers are to him. He singles out Ron Brown in particular – 'That's my best friend,' he says – for leading him to Shakespeare. 'I was a wounded spirit,' he tells the ladies, immediately breaking into his preacher cadence.

'Yeah,' they respond in unison, happy to be his congregation.

'And now I've been healed.'

'Oh yeah,' the women say.

'I feel like I was a caterpillar and now I'm a butterfly. I don't know if that sounds feminine or what, but I feel like I can fly now.' This is one of DeMond's standard lines, and it works as well on the KCIW women as it did on me. They smile and chuckle.

Sammie Byron (foreground) as Brutus, Ron Brown (center) as Cassius, and Jerry 'Big G' Guenthner (right corner) in the Julius Caesar *performance at Kentucky Correctional Institute for Women.*   Photo by Curt Tofteland

Shane's had enough of the competition and decides to put his hat in the ring. He stands up and addresses the women with outstretched arms. 'Ron Brown died and everyone "awwed," but as Cinna the Poet I took an ass-whooping right here and nobody "awwed" me! So could I get an "aww?"' All the women clap and say, "Aww." Shane grins. I look across the room at him and shake my head. He winks at me. Shameless.

'Are you also in college programs, in addition to Shakespeare?' the women ask.

Big G says that he would be, but, 'I already maxed-out college and got two degrees.'

DeMond interjects. 'I've got four,' he says, puffing out his chest.

Four? The women go crazy, clapping.

'A brother with four degrees?' says the woman behind me, enthusiastically. He told me they were diplomas, I think to myself.

The last question is directed toward Hal. 'How did you feel playing their wives, and what made you want to be those parts?' the women want to know.

Hal responds, 'Portia and Calpurnia are great characters. I played Prospero in 2003, so it was my turn to take a smaller part. Originally, I was just Calpurnia, but then the guy who played Portia was shipped, so I took on that role, too.'

'And thank you,' Hal adds, playing upon the women's anxiety at seeing two men behave as lovers, 'for all of your support when I was "giving it" to Brutus.' The women laugh nervously.

Tofteland interjects. 'For the guys in Shakespeare Behind Bars, it's a great honor to be able to play the female roles.' Tofteland asks the men who have played women's parts in the past to raise their hands. A half dozen hands go up. DeMond, Leonard, Hal, Marcel, Sammie, Ron. The women are surprised and delighted. Is it possible that Sammie Byron – the record-breaking weightlifting champion – has played a woman? Ron Brown – the Ja Rule look alike himself – has played a woman? 'Wooh!' shout the KCIW women, clapping and laughing.

After the talkback, as the men are packing up their equipment and the women are exiting the cafeteria, Towanda tugs on my arm.

'What did he do? When does he get out?' she begs.

'Which one?' I ask, although I needn't have.

'The beautiful one,' she says, pointing to Ron.

'He has life without parole for 25 years,' I reply.

'No!' Towanda protests.

'Hey, don't shoot the messenger,' I tell her.

Towanda laughs. 'Well, what about the light-skinned one?'

'I'm not sure,' I say. 'I think he's got a murder conviction, so, you know, it might be a while.'

Towanda looks at me with frustration as a prison guard tries to usher her out of the room.

'It was great to meet you,' I tell her.

She smiles. 'You too!' she says.

And then she lowers her voice and whispers to me, 'Thank you for sitting with us. I was so surprised that you wanted to sit with us. Most people are either afraid of us or they think we're scum, with us being locked up and all.'

Towanda's frank declaration touches my heart, and I fight back tears. 'Are you kidding?' I ask her. 'It was an honor.'

I watch as Towanda joins the other women, who are lined up like kindergarteners against the wall and told to walk, in rows, back to the door leading to the prison yard. Once Towanda reaches the door, she looks back and smiles at me one last time, before disappearing from sight.

'Unsex Me Here': Playing the Lady at Luckett

In my conversations with the Shakespeare Behind Bars actors, I come to learn that each man has a different reason for casting himself in the role of a woman. Some men, quite honestly, are forced to play a woman by older (and in most cases, considerably larger)

Shakespeare Behind Bars veterans like Big G and Sammie. Others offer to play a woman early on, to get it over with, as it were. Many of the men approach the process of choosing a Shakespeare role as an opportunity for personal growth; in their case, the character's sex doesn't matter as much as whether the character 'speaks' to them in some way. Some men choose to play a woman in order to challenge themselves to overcome their chauvinism. Some take the woman's part because they have committed crimes against women and see the opportunity to play a female victim as a fundamental component of their rehabilitation. And some of the men who identify with women like Desdemona and Lavinia do so, whether consciously or not, in part because they themselves have been emotionally, verbally, physically and sexually abused by men.

In DeMond Bush's case, he chose to play Tamora, Queen of the Goths, because he empathized with her loss when her two sons are killed by Titus Adronicus in the opening scene. 'I don't really think I picked Tamora,' DeMond tells me. 'I think Tamora called to me at the time. I had two children die, and I never really dealt with it. And Tamora sort of helped me. I felt and understood her anger, why she did what she did and why she would do what she wanted to do.'

During the rehearsal process, DeMond accidentally caught his bed on fire ('daggone cigarettes') and was sent to the Hole for several months. Leonard, who played Marcus, offered to play Tamora in DeMond's absence. DeMond kept his script with him in solitary, and learned both characters' lines. When DeMond was released just in time for the performance, he and Leonard 'decided to switch off of one another,' playing Marcus and Tamora on opposite nights.

'Did it take a lot of guts to play Tamora?' I ask Leonard. 'I mean, playing the woman means something different in prison, doesn't it?'

'Yes, yes,' Leonard says. 'And the reason I approached playing Tamora was for me, specifically, consciously, to confront those fears. Because for me of all the virtues I admire, courage is the greatest. Part of my recovery is my ability and willingness to live my life on my terms and being unconcerned about the unhealthy desire to have people always respect me and like me. I have to respect myself, I have to like myself, and I can't be concerned about what people think of me. So playing a woman was kind of extreme, but I wanted do that and to not be afraid of what people said because I knew that I could draw a lot out of Tamora. One of the things I wanted to achieve was not to layer on a transsexual femininity, not to change my voice, but to play her just as I would play any other character because I'm not playing 'a woman,' I'm playing someone who's been taken captive, I'm playing someone who's vying for power, I'm playing someone whoses sons were killed.'

'You're playing a human?' I suggest.

Leonard nods. 'I'm playing a human! Yes. Thank you. Because this is one thing that is very difficult. Most men in prison are misogynist. Most. And I would not say I'm misogynist, but I do have a certain level of arrogance and sexism still. And to me, for my own sake, I have to get beyond that. And like a lot of fears, they're really not as bad once you have the courage to confront them. And the reward was kind of having this little notch in my belt saying, "I played a woman's role. I played a woman's role in Shakespeare."'

'Does the woman's role eventually become a part of honor?' I ask.

'Yes,' Leonard says, 'it is for me. Actually, I would love to play Portia in *Merchant of Venice*. That is a very rich role. And it's so beautiful because here is a woman who is in such control, who is not the doormat wife, but has a marriage of equality. Plus that courtroom scene to me is just the greatest scene of all time, frankly.'

When I meet with Hal, he repeats Leonard's earlier claim. 'This prison is the most misogynistic place on the planet,' he says.

'Leonard told me the same thing,' I reply. 'Are some guys trying to pretend that it's not?'

Hal wrinkles up his nose. 'They tend to be very nice and polite around outside female visitors.'

'And then what do they say when I'm not around, Hal?'

He shuffles in his chair. 'That you're extremely nice.' And then he tells me the truth. 'On the first day you visited, the guys said, "I

didn't think she'd be so pretty. And that her boobs would be so big."
To be very blunt.'

I laugh. 'Well I wouldn't call that misogynistic. And anyway, my
girlfriends advised me to strap them down before I came in.'

'Breasts and buttocks are the eye-grabbers around here,' Hal
warns.

'Okay,' I ask him, 'If this is the most misogynistic place on earth,
are the men in the Shakespeare program less misogynistic than the
other inmates?

Hal thinks about my question for a minute before he says, 'On
the whole, I think they are.'

'It doesn't seem to me, from talking to the guys, that the women's
parts are necessarily the ones that nobody wants,' I point out. 'I
heard Leonard talk about Portia and how he would really love to
play that role. DeMond wants to play Lady Macbeth.'

Hal raises his eyebrows. I get the feeling that Hal has already
called dibs on Lady M. 'You know,' he says, 'when we do *Macbeth*,
there's going to be a big fight because a lot of the guys really want
to play Lady Macbeth.'

'But don't let them fool you,' Hal continues, 'it's a big challenge,
especially in this environment, to play a woman's role. Sammie had
to hide under the comedy to tackle it. He played Maria in *Twelfth
Night*.'

I ask Hal why he thinks Sammie wanted to play a woman.

Hal replies, 'I think Sammie just wanted to do it and get it out
of the way, and he thought that a comic character would be the easy
way to do it.'

'Is there an understanding that it's going to be every man's turn
to play a woman's role?' I ask.

'Yes, yes, yes,' Hal says. 'Last year with *The Tempest*, Red played
Miranda. And he did *not* want to play a woman's role and was just
kicking and screaming.'

I ask Marcel, nicknamed 'Red' because of his hair, 'When you
were choosing roles, did you want Miranda from the start?'

'No, I didn't!' Marcel exclaims. 'No way! What happened was a couple of guys, like G and Hal, said, "That role would fit you just right." I said, "Well, I don't wanna play no female role." After a while, we got to talking and they quoted lines to me, and then I started reading the part. I kinda fit me because it helped me to understand how me and my dad is, like how Miranda and Prospero are. After a while, I said, "Man, this character really fits me," after I read it for a couple of times and really got it down, deep down into me, and thought about it, and slept on it, and, you know, kind of meditated, and let it digest in me.'

'Why the hesitation?' I wonder. 'You said, "I don't wanna play no female role."'

Marcel stumbles. How is he supposed to answer this question without insulting me? 'Well, it's just that I didn't, at that time, I just didn't want to play a female role.'

'It must not be easy to play . . .' I begin.

Marcel cuts me off. 'Especially in prison. In a man's prison and stuff like that. But there wasn't nothing to it.'

'You didn't take any grief for it?' I ask. 'The guys didn't give you a hard time?'

'The guys just told me that I looked good,' Marcel says, 'and you know how guys are.'

'I do indeed.'

'They were just teasing me in a fun way,' he concludes.

'Did Ron play Ferdinand?' I ask him.

Marcel rolls his eyes. 'Yes. There was one guy who had it at first, but he got shipped, so Ron took the part. For me, in all honesty, Ron wouldn't have been my choice to be romantic with because I don't see nothing with him.'

I chuckle. 'Ron's not your ideal?'

'No,' Marcel responds.

'Who would you pick?' I ask.

Marcel thinks for a minute. 'That's hard. I'm pretty hard to please.'

'Sammie, maybe?' I volunteer.

Marcel shakes his head. 'No, nah. Not because of his size or nothing, it's just he wouldn't be my type. I would say probably Leonard. I like kind and gentle and things of that nature. But being strong, too, also, to tell me you're wrong and we need to work on these aspects of our relationship. Leonard is artistic, he's intelligent, he's funny. He's musical and things of that nature.'

'Do you feel as though you know what it feels like to be a woman?'

'In a sense,' Marcel says, 'yes, because I was taught by a woman, older than I was. She was just a friend, but she taught me how to please a woman, how to treat them, and respect them. Don't take them for granted. Sit and listen to them. Surprise them, sometimes, with things romantic. Plus, I sing. I sing to quite a few of my lady friends when I have the chance. That's what gives me more advantage than most guys.'

'So how do you feel,' I ask him, 'having this respect for women, when some of the guys that you're acting with are here because they've raped women or murdered women?'

I am taken aback by Marcel's answer. 'Well, I can't judge them guys because I really don't know the circumstances behind their crimes. Some women might have done cheated on their husbands. And they caught them in their house, in their bed or something and they just blanked out at that particular time.'

'That sounds like victim blaming to me, Red,' I interject.

'I'm not saying that it's right,' he protests, 'but some guys cannot take that type of pressure. Then I think it's a power struggle with some guys. Some guys want to control women because the guys have been rejected for so long or they've been abused.'

I raise my eyebrows.

'It's no excuse,' says Marcel, anticipating my objection. 'But these things play a part in it. And for the victim, I just feel sorry for them and if there's something I could do to comfort them, I would do it, even with the crime that I committed.'

'Which is?' I suddenly realize that I never pulled Marcel's record.

I might have spoken too soon in assuming he never committed a crime against a woman.

'I had a sexual abuse case,' Marcel admits. 'Well, I didn't sodomize anybody,' he protests. I never said he did.

Marcel continues, his eyes downcast. 'What I did, I snatched some money from three females and after I snatched the money, well . . . they were kind of older people. But at the time, I was on drugs, and I was like a wild man; I was out of control. I tried to stop, and I just couldn't.'

I sit in silence. Has Marcel just told me that he raped three elderly women? Marcel announces that he's recently completed the sex offenders program. I ask him what he's learned.

'They teach you how to keep yourself out of situations,' he tells me. 'If you're having a problem where you're going to rape a woman and you're alone, don't take drugs. Try to stay away from all that, or take a buddy with you when you go to see the woman.'

'What they're proposing sounds even more dangerous,' I respond. 'Take a buddy with you? What if you're both high and you both rape the woman? It sounds like they're teaching you avoidance.'

'Yes, avoid it until you're able to handle it,' Marcel says, as though he's reciting a mantra.

'But it's not feasible to avoid it forever,' I argue. 'There's going to be a time again when you have to make a choice.'

'Yes,' Marcel agrees, 'but to make a rational decision you have to be off substances. Then you can say, "No I don't want to go rape a woman because I know they'll send me to prison."'

I shake my head in disbelief at the prison system's approach to rehabilitating sex offenders. No wonder many Luckett inmates find the Shakespeare program more beneficial than their institutionalized forms of treatment. Indeed, for some inmates who have committed crimes against women, Shakespeare affords them a unique opportunity for therapeutic role-playing. Certainly the most publicized instance of an inmate using Shakespeare as an occasion to examine his crime against a woman is that of Sammie Byron in the 1999 *Othello*, but when I meet with Mike Smith, who played Desdemona in the same production, I find that Mike had similar reasons for taking the role.

But it's not in prison that I interview Mike, oh no. I meet with Mike at an upscale Louisville restaurant. One of Shakespeare Behind Bars' proudest 'alums,' Mike served out his time in 2000. Since then, he has fallen in love, married, and established a successful career as a manager of a dry cleaners. But he still remembers the crimes he committed, and he still remembers the eight years and ten months he spent in prison as a result. In 1992, as Mike tells the story, he had just graduated from high school and was unhappy at home. Though he told his mother and his 'distant and stern,' borderline-alcoholic, military father that he was sinking deeper into depression, they ignored his worries. One night, Mike snapped, and pulled a kitchen knife on his girlfriend and her mother. He was convicted of first- and second-degree assault. In 1999, one year before his release, Mike asked to play the role of Desdemona so that he could better empathize with his victims.

'To take on the challenge of a woman's role takes courage,' Mike tells me. 'I mean, I'm not ashamed to call it courage. To say, "Hey, I'm gonna do it. I can do it. Laugh if you want to." It was a big step for me. And, really, we all use that as a mile marker or stepping stone, you know. "When are you gonna do the woman's role," you know? "When are you ready for that?" When we all say we're ready to take that step, it's kind of like saying, "Hey, I'm ready to go to that next level. I'm ready to get out there and put it all on the line."'

No matter how enlightened the Shakespeare Behind Bars participants might be, many of them still see the action of playing the women's parts as a sacrifice. When Big G describes Mike's willingness to play Desdemona, he says that Mike 'took the hit' for Sammie. Mike explains that for most inmates, it's not that they're afraid of playing a woman necessarily; it's that they're afraid of being perceived as homosexual. 'I was comfortable doing it because I had been there so long and knew everybody and everybody knew that, you know, uhh . . . that it wasn't my way of life, you know?'

'You mean being gay, or what do you mean?' I ask him.

'Yeah, yeah,' he says.

'In my case,' Mike continues, 'I knew that I had to go ahead and take the risk because in taking the role of Desdemona I was seeking something as far as my rehabilitation. I thought maybe if I played Desdemona I could start to understand how my victims felt. At the time, there was no way I could imagine. Really, when I thought about playing a woman's role, I thought, "If ever, then it's got to be Desdemona. There's no other choice." I thought, of all the women's parts, I could really take something from this one. Sammie is just so overpowering and can be a monster. And he brought Othello and the whole scene to a level where it was intimidating, really. And I tried to pull something from that experience just to look into a man's eyes and see that anger and to not know what's about to transpire. I just needed to experience what it was like to be in that position.'

Though Mike says that playing Desdemona was helpful for his rehabilitation, he also acknowledges the limits of any form of therapy and recognizes the difference between pretending to be a victim and actually being one. 'I had a mixed reaction to playing Desdemona,' he says. 'There was a part of me where I felt I could connect with my victims more, but at the same time I said to myself, "There's no way I can know the full impact that I had." The fact is that after the show was over, it was all done.' For the women who survived his assault, however, Mike says, 'There's no way of ending it or fixing it. The emotional damage and the fear that I caused, I'm responsible for that. If they go outside or if they hear something or if there's a time that they're startled more than they should be, well, who's responsible for that? Me. So I mean there's really no way I can fix that, so I can't imagine what it's like for them.'

Like his friend Mike Smith, Ron Brown purports to have a great deal of sympathy for women. 'I've never committed a crime against a woman out of all of the things that I've done wrong,' he tells me, and his tone of voice suggests he thinks it's the only thing that makes him human. 'A lot of my respect comes from having grown up in a house with all women – my sisters and my mother, and I have a tremendous respect for them – but even more than that, I have two daughters and I can't imagine how I'd feel if something happened to them.' Ron is particularly defensive of Shakespeare's Lavinia. 'What happens to Lavinia just really, really bothers me to my soul,' he says. 'And it could have to do with my own sexual abuse when I was younger, but it bothers me.'

'With Lavinia,' Ron explains, 'the way I theorized it is she represents all females. She was raped and she had her hands and tongue cut out. In many ways, that's what's happened to the female gender. Over the course of history, women have been economically, socially and, in some cases, physically raped. But Lavinia isn't even able to speak about it. After a while she gets to the point where she can take the stick between her nubs and write it down, but even then she has to depend on men to be able to understand and translate exactly what she is saying. Lavinia has no choice but to depend on the people around her. A lot of times what women do in those situations is blame themselves so they don't even know how to name their perpetrator. Even when they are able to speak it, they're still dependent on men to translate and understand what they're saying. Some guys may know it, but they'll say to the woman, "You're looking at your own name written there because you've contributed to it."'

Though he accepted the role of Emilia back in 1999 in order to get the obligation of playing a woman out of the way, Ron looks forward to the day when Shakespeare Behind Bars produces *The Taming of the Shrew*. His eyes brighten just thinking of it.

'Initially, if I was gonna play a female role I wanted to play Kate,' he says. 'Kate is my second favorite character in Shakespeare, behind Hamlet. I like Kate. I remember seeing *Taming of the Shrew* when I was like 11 or 12, and then I used to watch *Moonlighting*, and they had a story based on it. And the personality of Kate was so intriguing to me. I like the strength that she had, and I like the back and forth that they had in the relationship. It wasn't something that was like a fairytale thing. It was a battle that they were going through, and it was like, "Okay, at some point both parties have to make concessions."'

I ask Ron what he thinks of the end of the play, Kate's 'submission speech,' as some people call it.

'See, I don't see it like that,' Ron says. 'I think it's like he doesn't even care about winning the bet at that point, so the point of it is ∴ . . it represented love to me because if you love somebody it's not about what you want, it's about what the other person wants, so they represented love in its purest sense to me, and it's basically saying, "I will put myself second to you", and if you have two people in a relationship who are willing to say, "Okay, all I want to do is love you, regardless of what you're doing in return", well, loving somebody without thinking about what the return is gonna be is something that's kind of a lost art.'

Some months later, Jean Trounstine, author of *Shakespeare Behind Bars: The power of drama inside one women's prison*, invites me to her home to watch video recordings of ten years' worth of theatre productions at Framingham Women's Prison in Massachusetts. In addition to several non-Shakespearean plays, including *Lysistrata*, *Waiting for Lefty*, *Simply Maria*, *The Scarlet Letter*, and *Arsenic and Old Lace*, Trounstine shows me videos of the women's prison adaptations of *The Merchant of Venice* and, Ron's favorite, *The Taming of the Shrew*.

The Framingham prison women's reading of Shakespeare's play is slightly different from Mr Brown's rather romantic one. Indeed, the Framingham *Rapshrew*, as they call it, is an excellent example of the Framingham group's characteristic method of adapting Shakespeare by rewording and updating the text and adding a decidedly feminist spin. In place of the Christopher Sly induction, for instance, Trounstine's group substitutes three female rappers, 'The Shrews', who, in their song 'Rollin' with the Shrews' seek to reclaim traditionally derogatory terms like 'shrew' and 'bitch.' In Trounstine's video, The Shrews' rap is an invocation to the women inmates in the audience:

> How do you identify a shrew?
> How can you tell if the name is true?
> Here's the test: anybody say to you
> 'Don't nag, don't sass, don't gimme no lip.
> Don't bitch, don't cuss?'
> Well, sing it, honey, 'cause you're one of us!

> I'm a shrew, I'm a shrew, I'm a shrew, She's a shrew, I'm a shrew!

It's not until the end of the song that The Shrews even mention Kate and Petruchio, renamed 'Truck' in this production. The rappers announce, 'This guy named Shakespeare, he told it first. | But we're gonna tell it in our own kind of verse.' Throughout the play, The Shrews reappear, like a Greek Chorus led by Medea, bound to undermine any trace of sexism that might exist in Shakespeare's play. In response to the scene in which Petruchio denies Kate a dress and hat, for example, The Shrews say:

> You know it makes a shrew see red
> When a guy won't live up to what he said.
> Kate says, 'This is goin' too far.
> Who needs you? I got Mastercard.'
> 'I'll buy it myself,' she tells the clerk.
> 'And by the way, Truck, I'm goin' to work.'

At the end of the play, after Kate 'submits' to Petruchio, The Shrews reprise their 'Rollin' With The Shrews' song, including the remarkable first verse.

> How old were you when you started to think you
>   might be a shrew?

I was just thirteen.
Guy came on to me, and I whipped out my blade –
You know, my tongue – I cut him bad.
Yeah, boy!
I gave him the unkindest cut. You cut him there?
No, no not there!
Hey! Listen! Didn't you hear?
They say the doctors have just figured out
What shrews have always known without a doubt.
Why it scares a man just to hear a shrew talk
'cause a man's most sensitive part is his heart!
Yeah, boy!

In the video of the performance, by the end of the rap, the women inmates in the audience are standing on their feet, waving their hands and shouting along with the actors, 'I'm a shrew! She's a shrew! I'm a shrew!' And next to the stage, clapping and laughing along with the women inmates, is Jean Trounstine.

Rapshrew: Jean Trounstine and the Framingham Women's Prison

There are two names that spring to mind when one thinks of women's prison theatre directors. One is Rhodessa Jones, founder of The Medea Project: Theatre for Incarcerated Women. The other is Jean Trounstine. Both women began their programs in the late 1980s, both believe in the arts as a forum for social activism, both have a keen awareness of the issues that are specific to women inmates, and both are resolute and passionate in their efforts to empower incarcerated women. Though Trounstine's program inside Framingham is now defunct due to lack of administrative support and funding, she still works with probationary women and has founded a program entitled Changing Lives through Literature, in which Massachusetts' offenders are sentenced to participate in a literature class rather than serve time in jail.

When I meet up with Trounstine in January 2006, we both have recently attended the Modern Language Association meeting where we participated in the 'Prison Shakespeare' panel and watched the screening of the *Shakespeare Behind Bars* documentary about Tofteland's program. The film has been on Jean's mind. Having worked with incarcerated women for ten years, she is eager to talk about the differences between Curt's program and hers. When I sit down to interview her, one of the first things she mentions is that her women actors were better at playing men than Curt's male actors are at playing women.

'Women watch men more,' she explains. 'Women know how men move. We know how they look. We know how to disguise ourselves as men. Also, there's a freedom when a woman plays a man that comes from being your aggressive, assertive self that you're not allowed to be in real life. That's vibrant, that's enlivening. It's exactly the opposite for men playing women's parts. For a man playing a woman, it's a big deal because it's not something you'd ever *want* to be. For a woman playing a man, it's a big deal because it's not something you're *allowed* to be.'

I ask Jean to compare her prison Shakespeare program with other programs across the country.

'When I began my program,' Jean says, 'Theatre in general was more important than, necessarily, Shakespeare. One of the Framingham women, Dolly, wanted to do a play because the men's prison had a theatre group. So my first objective was to give the women something that would make them feel more equal. Women are treated like such idiots in prison. It's as though their lives don't exist. I wanted to do something that would help them be heard. And our method of adapting Shakespeare into their own words developed out of that because it was a way for them to understand the language. When they put Shakespeare into their own words, it made more sense. And they owned it.'

'Is that part of your feminist approach to Shakespeare,' I ask her, 'to make the women feel empowered in that they're re-wording this great male poet?'

She nods. 'Yes, but it wasn't part of my original plan to adapt the text, that whole process just developed naturally. I think it sprang from my innate sense that they needed to make it belong to them. I wanted the women to be successful. And the notion that they had to get Shakespeare 'right', intellectually, was really not helpful. It wasn't a competition.'

She continues. 'That's another thing that's different between women and men. You could see in the way Shakespeare Behind Bars conduct their rehearsals that there's a competition between the men. One guy gets up and does his lines, and the other guys are yelling, "Come on! Do it!" It's almost "Sports Shakespeare." They have a huddle right before the show whereas we women are doing a relaxation exercise and trying to connect to ourselves and each other. I think if it had been all about learning Shakespeare's language it would've scared the women off. The Framingham women are just like you and me except they're not privileged.'

'You say that these women are just like you and me,' I reply, 'but in your book, you write about them with a kind of reverence which suggests that you don't think these women are necessarily like you and me, that there's something even more heroic about them, to your mind. In your Introduction, you say, "There's something about a woman who dares to get in trouble that has always been close to my heart", and one of Bertie's last lines when she's playing Pearl in *The Scarlet Letter* is, "Crime and punishment are for those with nerves of iron, and ordinary people cannot endure it."'

'I think the women were risk-takers in a *bad* way,' Jean distinguishes, 'and I think theatre allowed them to take risks in a *good* way. I admire their risk-taking ability. I like people who think outside the box. That is why I think I connected with them, because they weren't afraid in certain ways, like a lot of people, a lot of women, are. A lot of the Framingham women were feisty. I'm like that. I've always not liked boundaries, and I respect not liking boundaries. It means that you can question and think for yourself, and there's a potential to really affect a person when they're able to question and think.'

I smile at Jean's description of herself and sneak a peak at the clock on the wall. It's almost midnight. Jean and I have spent the entire day together; we've talked about prison Shakespeare and watched video after video of the Framingham productions for almost 14 hours straight. I'm exhausted, frankly. But Jean seems to have a boundless supply of energy.

'Based on what you've just said about questioning authority and thinking outside the box,' I tell her, 'I can't imagine what the Framingham administrators, who are in charge of managing what happens *in* the box, the box that is their prison, as it were, must've thought about a woman like you, a woman who says, "I've always not liked boundaries", and means it, lives it.'

We both chuckle. 'I was always getting in trouble for something, always,' she confesses. The warden sat me down one time and said, "If it weren't for the fact that you do really good work you would be out of here." As much as he was a pain in the ass, he was my defender, and when he was gone, that's when lot of things went to hell.'

I draw Jean's attention to a comment she made while we were watching the *Scarlet Letter* video. 'When Hester is led away in chains at the end your play, you said, "That was amazing that we were allowed to get the correctional officer's outfit."'

She rolls her eyes as if to reenact her initial response. 'It was a really big deal. They didn't like it that an inmate was playing a corrections officer.'

'It reminds me of Shakespeare's day when the city authorities were threatened by the actors dressing up as kings, or dressing above their station,' I suggest.

Jean nods. 'It was *exactly* that. We had the same trouble when the women portrayed the police in *Arsenic and Old Lace*.'

'But are the officers not paying any attention to any scenes other than those?' I ask. 'Because the plays you choose are remarkably subversive.'

'I know,' she says triumphantly.

'Right?' I repeat. 'And purposefully so.'

Jean thinks about it and tries to qualify her initial exuberance. 'Well, I don't know if I would say subversive. I definitely have an anti-establishment streak. The question of "What is justice?" is the reason I was so attracted to *The Merchant of Venice*. Shylock obviously takes justice into his own hands. And then the Christian world takes justice into their hands and takes away his religion. I think prison is a horrible thing. And the plays that I choose definitely are about questioning authority. But I don't know that I would say they're subversive. I mean, there was no riot after any play.'

'But there are riots *in* the plays,' I remind her. 'And the women inmates in the audience respond to *Waiting for Lefty* by shouting "Strike!" and waving their fists in the air. During the question and answer time, I hear inmates questioning the prison authorities and other inmates agreeing with them. They are very vocal about their discontent – in front of the officers and guards and visitors – and the vehicle, the venue for them expressing their discontent, is your play.'

'It wasn't like I wanted the women to go and overturn the prison, though,' Trounstine insists. 'I wanted the women to believe they could take control over their lives. And, yes, if that meant standing up and writing a letter saying "I deserve to get out of here", that was the kind of empowerment that I was looking for, not for them to necessarily overthrow the government. So I think the word subversive would've been a prison word. The prison would've called me subversive, as opposed to calling me, say, empowering. I mean, I did a couple of things, probably, that were not kosher, so to speak. I did enjoy every time I was able to get past security and keep my gold necklace on by hiding it underneath my sweater. I felt like I had achieved something every time I snuck it past. And that was the way that prison made you feel, like you were small, so much was prohibited. It's a horrible, horrible idea, that deprivation helps anyone change their life.'

'What should we do, instead of locking people up?' I ask.

'Well,' she replies, 'I think there are probably some people who have to be locked up. But there are a lot of people who don't. We need to expand our probation and mentorship programs. And there are lots of programs like the Changing Lives through Literature program, lots of alternative programs, in which people are supervised but not incarcerated.'

'What did you learn from the women?' I ask her.

'Hmm,' Jean thinks. 'Well, beyond everything else, that I could stay doing it for ten years. I mean, there aren't many people who last; people only do it for a year or two.'

'So you learnt about the stamina of your soul,' I say.

Jeans nods her head. 'Yes. And also that I was willing to adapt myself, and my loud mouth and intense personality, and I was willing to adapt everything in order to go in there for those women. And I do think that the force of my good work is what kept me there. And it kept me there until the system just became so much larger than anything my work could touch. I started to be harder and harder to get my plays approved. I had wanted to do a play about sexual abuse, but they told me that sexual abuse wasn't a good play to do in prison, or some bullshit like that. They didn't want me to talk about racism and classism. I did. They always called me and said, "Don't talk about anything controversial. Don't talk about things that could get them stirred up."'

She gets excited just thinking about it. 'I didn't talk about anything controversial necessarily, intellectually,' Jean says. 'But, you know,' she winks at me, 'that's what literature does. You read a play, and you think.'

Act 5

A Visit with Warden Larry Chandler

One of the most talented actors from amongst Trounstine's alumnae is Rhonda, the woman who played Portia in the 1988 Framingham production of *The Merchant of Venice*. In her book *Shakespeare Behind Bars: The power of drama inside a women's prison*, Trounstine recounts a conversation that she listened in on when Rhonda was walking out of a rehearsal with her fellow inmate and girlfriend, Lynn. Trounstine writes, 'On my way out of the classroom, I overhear Rhonda say to Lynn, "This play is controlling me better than all the tricks the Department of Corrections has ever had up its sleeve"' (p. 152). I ask Jean to respond to the philosophy implicit in Rhonda's statement, the idea that Shakespeare can be a more effective disciplinary force than traditional institutional means.

'I think it just speaks to the fact that what really works for people is when they're motivated to do something for themselves,' Trounstine replies. 'And Rhonda was smart enough to know that a lot of what people tried to get her to do in prison was just childish, garbage-y, pass-the-time activities. The play was really something that kept her out of trouble, in a certain way. She wanted to be in the play, so she didn't want to do anything to screw up. Rhonda was a con. And she couldn't be a con when it came to the play. She had to be there. She had to be responsible. She was finally holding herself accountable. Being a part of the play modified her behavior.'

There are many activities in prison that are meant to keep inmates in conformity and to distract them from causing trouble.

Sports. Church services. These activities, while they might be liberating or freeing to a certain extent, also serve a very practical function for the prison in that they help to keep the inmates complacent and under control. According to the inmates, Shakespeare is one of these activities. Several of the men at Luckett attest to the behavioral modification effect of the Shakespeare Behind Bars program. 'Shakespeare helps me to conform,' Leonard Ford says. 'To remember what's expected, to cooperate with people, to respect authority, to love one another, to support one another, to work toward a goal.' Big G credits the Shakespeare Behind Bars program for the relatively low number of violent crimes at Luckett. 'I take a lot of pride in what goes on in the yard as far as it not being violent, you know,' he says. 'I take pride in being able to reach out to young guys and help them keep their head on. This whole prison is changing. They say one bad apple can spoil the whole bunch; one good apple can help a whole barrel of rotten ones. When I first got locked up, guys, older convicts, told me how to bring dope into prison and how to be a loan shark. Those of us in Shakespeare, we wanna change direction of ourselves and that's why we don't have a lot of murders on the yard and a lot of rapes and killings.'

Anyone who is concerned that prison Shakespeare directors are secretly working for the establishment needn't worry. As Trounstine's case suggests, those who become involved with Shakespeare in the correctional system are usually theatre practitioners or university professors, many who have volunteered their time for years, who regard their work in Corrections as one aspect of their commitment to social activism. Prison Shakespeare directors see the theatre as a place of freedom, social activism, and even revolution. To them, Shakespeare provides inmates with opportunities for personal liberation in spite of institutional restrictions.

But what does Shakespeare mean to Department of Corrections employees? Is Shakespeare the equivalent of buying another set of dumbbells for the gymnasium – just another activity to pass the time and allow the inmates to release frustration? Larry Chandler is the warden at Kentucky State Reformatory, just a few miles down the road from Luther Luckett Correctional Complex, where he served as warden from 1999–2003. During his time at Luckett, the Shakespeare Behind Bars group performed some of their most challenging plays: *Titus Andronicus*, *Othello*, *Hamlet* and *The Tempest*. If there's any warden who's qualified to talk about prison Shakespeare, it's Chandler.

However, I almost don't get a chance to meet with him. When I arrive at the Kentucky State Reformatory on the day of our scheduled interview, prompt for my 2pm appointment, which I confirmed in advance with the warden himself, I'm not on the guest list. The guard at the gate phones up to the warden's secretary. I'm not in the warden's diary either. She phones back in about ten minutes to say that I can come up anyway. When I finally meet up with Larry Chandler, he's on his way out of his office, ostensibly to look for one of his medical staff. He's pretty busy, but he's willing to talk while we walk. He leads me on a tour of the Kentucky State Reformatory.

'Did I surprise you?' I say as I shake Chandler's hand. 'I had trouble getting in because they said I didn't have an appointment with you.'

'I forgot to tell them,' Chandler grumbles, charging down the hallway. There was a thunderstorm the night before which had knocked the power out for three hours. He's had more important things than a silly interview on his mind. 'I read the interview questions you emailed me,' he says. 'Your one question is way off base and kind of ludicrous. I mean, that sounds to me like an inmate who has an exaggerated self-worth.'

'Which question is that?' I ask, trying to keep up with him as he walks down one corridor and through the prison infirmary.

'"Would the parole board deny parole because they thought that an inmate controlled the institution?" The answer is no.'

'But that isn't really the question that I asked,' I remind Chandler. 'What I asked was,' I say, pulling out my list of questions and reading from it, '"The guys who have been in the Shakespeare program for several years take a huge amount of pride in being decent men and good role models in their everyday behavior. Aren't 'good inmates' like Sammie Byron absolutely necessary to keep a prison running in conformity and do you think that there's any parole board mindset that would say – maybe not even consciously – that men like Sammie Byron need to stay around because the prison wouldn't run as smoothly without them?"' That's a darn good question, I think to myself.

Chandler marches forward but glares at me out of the corner of his eye. He doesn't answer my question. Reporters! Who needs 'em? Now even college professors are turning into the damn press corps. And they never get the story right. 'You know,' he says, 'one of the things that we probably don't do well in Corrections is inform the public what Corrections is all about. Everyone wants to tell me how to run this place.'

As we near the psychiatric ward, Chandler calls out to one employee, 'Thomas, thanks for coming in last night.'

'You're welcome,' Thomas says.

Encouraged by Chandler's politeness – toward Thomas, at least – I try again. 'So should we go to some of the questions that didn't offend you?' I suggest.

'Well, I'm not offended,' Chandler grunts at me. 'The one question was a little naïve. Twenty-six years, nothing offends me.'

'I also asked a question about educational programs in prison,' I volunteer.

Chandler is willing to talk about education. 'Every study that's been published in the last ten years indicates that education has one of the most positive impacts on recidivism,' he tells me. 'I can *force* you into education and it still has a positive impact on your recidivism. Here at KSR, we have a film studio and make educational programs and force-feed them to the inmates.' And then the warden starts asking me the questions.

'So your interest in Shakespeare Behind Bars is because you're a Shakespeare scholar?'

'That's right,' I say. 'What I'm doing is . . .'

Chandler interrupts. 'Have you met Curt?'

'Oh, yeah,' I tell Chandler.

'If Curt was teaching crocheting it'd be a successful program,' the warden says.

'That's right,' I agree. 'The men at Luckett think of him as a father figure.'

'They sing his praises,' Chandler says, breaking into a smile.

'They just love him,' I say.

'Right,' Chandler nods. Finally something we agree on.

'And in many cases they credit him with saving their lives,' I tell the warden.

Chandler shakes his head. 'Oh, but that has yet to be seen. The real test comes when we open the gate and push them out. I mean, it's all artificial in here, you have to understand that; it's all artificial. Our job is to prepare them for that day when they leave. That's the test of success. And we may never know whether we did a good job or not. If we hear about it, it's because we failed. Jerry Guenthner and Sammie Byron are high-profile crimes. The press has a field day with them. When we did *Titus*, you know, Guenthner's a cop killer. I had a local television station interview me, and the first question out of their mouths was, "How can you justify such a violent program?" Then I guess I'd have to stop teaching the Old Testament.'

I laugh. Did the warden just make a joke?

'That's right,' I say. 'I actually asked the guys about why they thought Curt chose some of the most violent plays to do. They say that it has to do, basically, with catharsis.'

Chandler shakes his head. 'It has to do with their lives,' he tells me. '*Their lives.*'

Chandler gestures to someone behind a glass box, and the huge security-controlled door we are standing in front of begins to rumble open.

'You're about to enter the Kentucky Psychiatric Treatment,' he announces. 'It's kind of a misnomer.'

'How so?' I ask.

The warden looks at me like I'm stupid. 'This place rocks and rolls.'

I follow Chandler into the psychiatric ward, a large rectangular space about 100 feet long. There are two floors. Each floor has 25 cells, one inmate per cell. A medical team comprised of a man and a woman dressed in white gowns are taking a cart full of little pill containers around the ward. About a dozen inmates are standing up behind the steels doors, their faces glued to the small six-inch by six-inch windows, peering out. They don't look at me for a second. They're staring straight at the cart. There's no way to open the thick, steel doors of the cells manually. The man in the white coat opens one of the tiny windows and calls through the thick glass, 'Do you want your medicine?' In other cells, one inmate nods; another grunts; another pounds his fist to the window. If the inmate that the man is addressing responds, I can't tell. The man opens a tiny latched door, where a doorknob would usually be, and slides in the medicine, like a banker giving a customer her money. When the little door opens, I glimpse inside the cell. It's entirely cement. Even the bed . . . well, there is no bed; there's just a long cement block, raised about a foot off the floor. The inmate doesn't have a shirt on, and I can't see the rest of his body, but it's possible that he's entirely naked. He sits on the hard floor, lifeless. There is no toilet. There is nothing. This is worse than any depiction of prison I've ever seen on television or film. *Silence of the Lambs*, *Oz*; this is worse. And the thing that makes it worse, even more striking than the pathetic state of the inmates, is the smell. The psychiatric ward smells like death.

'Quite a tour,' I tell Chandler, and I'm starting to realize that it's not just because he's looking for one of his medical staff that the warden has brought me to the psychiatric ward. Chandler wants me to see this. He trusts me enough, member of the press though I may be, to show me the very worst part of his prison.

'These are 50 of the worst,' he says, as if he read my mind. 'When we have various incidents it usually kicks off right here. We were without power last night for several hours until about three in the morning. Fortunately, we made it through without any of these guys hanging themselves.'

Chandler reveals this information as if he's telling me that he's running low on breakfast cereal. He's so nonchalant that it takes me a while to comprehend what he's saying. 'Wow,' I say. 'When you're without power does that mean that . . .?'

'There were no lights other than emergency lights. We had to double up on staff and put one on each floor to make sure that they were looking in routinely.'

'Could you still get the doors open and shut?' I ask. The warden looks at me like I'm an idiot. Again.

'You would not want to open the doors,' he tells me. 'That's the whole point.'

'The door never gets open, is that what you're saying?'

'In some situations it does, under very controlled circumstances.'

'Wow.'

'Very controlled circumstances.'

'Wow. So for how long are they in there?'

'It depends on the individual and the kind of treatment they need. Sometimes they never get out.'

'Wow.'

'We'll try looking for Mark on the other side,' Chandler says, and we start to walk to another wing of the prison to look for the doctor.

'I'm a prison warden who doesn't believe in prisons,' Chandler tells me as we retrace our steps through the infirmary. 'We've got over two million people in prison, and it's not working. I mean, this is a difficult classroom, to put people in prison for 20, 30 years and then to open the door. You have to make the atmosphere as positive as possible and you have to make opportunities available. And then some of them you have to brush aside. Some of them you give up on.'

'Some of them aren't going to get it?' I ask.

Chandler nods. 'Just get out of the way. Shut the hell up. Go sit in the cell. And then work with the rest of them. That's kind of a hard view, but I'm sorry. There's 1,900 people in this institution, I can't . . . And we're going to push positive attitudes. And if you don't have one, whether you're staff or whether you're an inmate, if you don't believe in our mission statement, get the hell out of the way. Move it.'

Outside the infirmary, the warden passes an inmate who is sitting on a window seat. 'Are you lost?' Chandler challenges him. The inmate laughs and breaks into the hymn 'Amazing Grace': 'I once was lost but now am found; | 'Twas blind but now I see.'

Chandler points me down another hallway. 'That was the psychiatric side; this is the bad boy's side. These are just inmates,' he says, leading the way.

We arrive on the scene of a mess. In this section of the prison, the inmates are housed in barred cells. It's very dark. I look down the corridor. Evidently, there's been a riot. Plastic cups and wrappers litter the narrow hallway that runs between the cells. You couldn't walk down the corridor without stepping on trash; there's a sea of debris at least six inches high. There's liquid all over the floor. The place smells like urine.

'They're cleaning it up now,' the officer on duty tells the warden. 'That's good,' Chandler says.

'They had a problem last night,' the officer explains. 'One officer didn't want to deliver the mail. And the inmates got mad and started throwing stuff on the walk.'

The warden says, 'Well, I was here at about three o'clock in the morning, and the riot didn't have anything to do with mail.'

The officer says, 'I talked to most of the inmates and they said that they was mad at the officer before the power went off and that's when they trashed the walk.'

Chandler instructs the officer to talk to the inmates and the officers about the matter again so that he can get his story straight. We turn around and walk out.

On the way out, the warden says to another employee, 'Have you got enough beds?'

The employee says, 'No, I don't.'

'How many beds you got?' Chandler asks.

The employee says, 'Right now I'm full. I'm cutting people out based upon time they've served; it's kind of chaotic at the moment.'

The warden then addresses the lieutenant, 'Lieutenant, I see you identified one of the culprits.' The lieutenant responds, 'One of them. Two of them are black, and in one case, the officers think they got the wrong one. It's his roommate.'

'Just be fair,' Warden Chandler cautions the lieutenant.

The lieutenant says, 'I'm going to kick out the one, but the other can stay.'

Chandler leads me up the stairs and into a meeting room where he finally finds the medical staff member he was looking for. He whispers something in his ear. Five seconds later we're ready to head to his office.

'Did you want to become a warden when you were a kid?' I ask Chandler once he's seated behind his desk.

'No,' he laughs. 'What kid sets out to become a warden? But my uncle was a jailer for years and he retired, and in those days, one of the requirements for being the jailer was that you lived within 1,000 feet of the jail. Well, I was the only one who wanted the job. I thought it would just be to kind of get me by for a while. That was in 1982, and I've been in Corrections ever since.

'You must've learned a lot from your uncle jailer.'

Chandler nods. 'I think I learned respect. And that's part of our core values; that's right on top. Discipline and respect. I mean, he was a one-man show and he operated it successfully, I think, because he treated his inmates with respect, but with discipline.'

'What do you see happening to prisons in the next 10 or 20 years?' I ask.

'I think a couple of things ought to happen,' Chandler replies. 'I think education ought to be mandatory. If legislature can say that 50 years is mandatory, let's make it contingent on education. Education works, and that's proven statistically. And I think religion works, but that's so hard to measure. I'm not a deeply religious person, but I've seen people that profess a belief in God that I have never seen once they get out. And that may be because they have a church supporting them once they're out.'

I tell the warden the many of the men in the Shakespeare group say that they find a spirituality in Shakespeare.

'Shakespeare's language reaches down into your soul,' he says.

'What about you and Shakespeare?' I ask. 'Do you like Shakespeare?'

Chandler nods. 'I like some of it. And, of course, I like all the popular stuff. I've got maybe two or three collections of Shakespeare, and I'll sit down and read it occasionally, but I'm not a big Shakespeare fan.'

'Are you a fan of the Shakespeare Behind Bars program, though?' I presume. 'I've heard that it's one of the most successful programs at Luckett.'

But Chandler is reluctant to overestimate the program. 'From a warden's point of view, if you measure Shakespeare by how it impacts the institution, the program is successful for two reasons. It keeps things quiet and provides opportunity.' So my earlier question wasn't naïve, I think to myself: one of the primary functions of Shakespeare absolutely is that it keeps the prison running smoothly.

'Plus,' Chandler continues, still speaking in his administrative capacity, 'We get so much good press from Shakespeare. And I thought it was important to plant the seed for other institutions to follow our lead and to let people know that we can entertain ourselves. I mean, Shakespeare is cheap entertainment. That's the warden in me saying to other wardens, "I know you'll like Shakespeare because it's something for your prison population that's going to occupy their time, it's going to create some positive talk, and it's not going to cost you a dime." I think my job is to try to put as many educational opportunities out there as possible.'

'You've used the words "education" and "teaching" more than any others during the time I've talked to you,' I point out. 'I'm a professor,' I say, 'but I think most professors don't think of what wardens do as teaching, possibly because that would make our institutions look too similar.' Chandler laughs. 'Do you think prisons are like universities?' I ask.

'I think they can be and probably should be,' he says. 'I believe in learning. I believe it to my very toes.'

'You know, speaking of being a professor,' Chandler continues, 'a good friend of mine is a professor at University of Louisville in Criminal Justice, and he teaches all the theory and thinks it's easy to be a warden, and I think he lives in a dream world. You can teach theory until you're blue in the face. I know how I'm gonna run the place. If everything is equal, you ought to listen to me. I'm the one who's done it.'

He goes on. 'But the public needs to understand what prison is all about. After 24 years, I still believe in people. No matter what they've done, no matter what mistakes these men have made, life goes on. One of the tough parts of this job is that people bring the victim into it, but that's not my job. As heinous as some of the crimes are; in here, I deal with the 1,900 inmates who committed those crimes, not with those who the crimes were committed against. Our job is to make a difference in the inmates' lives so that there are no more victims. That's a hard sell to the public. These people don't come in here, like the Quakers thought in the early 1700s, and sit and pray around the Bible and repent. Life takes on some sense of normalcy, even in this strange environment, and I wish the public would understand that.'

'So,' I say, 'society has a responsibility to treat ex-offenders that they come into contact with as people. Give them a chance to work for them, for instance.'

Chandler nods. 'If you believe in the system on the front end, you have to believe in the system at the tail end. I mean, they have paid their debt. And I'm not sure if the public's ready for that.'

The warden leans back in his chair and shakes his head. 'And what a disadvantage. Imagine. I'm trying to recall what Guenthner's sentence is. I think it's life, but he has an opportunity for parole. Say he does 40 years and walks out. What a disadvantage. I mean, not only does he have to overcome things that you've taken for granted for the last 40 years, but he walks into a new world, and it may not be a brave new world, and he's walking out with that "cop-killer" tag on him, unless he just fades into the woodwork somehow. Think of how difficult that is. And what a lot of courage that takes.'

'I have not seen a truly evil person in my life,' Chandler concludes. 'If I did, he had me fooled. But I've never met a Ted Bundy or somebody like that. I've met Jerry Guenthner and Sammie Byron. They've done horrible, horrible things. And they should pay for their crimes – don't misunderstand me; people should pay for their crimes – but I'm not sure that prison is where they should pay for them.'

Desdemona Speaks: Mike Smith on the Outside

Mike Smith is someone who knows the disadvantages ex-offenders face when they are released back into society after being incarcerated for years and years. Mike makes a decent living working at a dry cleaners, but he has to put in 70 to 80 hours per week for a boss who uses his knowledge of Mike's criminal history as a threat that he could fire him at any minute. Though Mike has been trying to find another position, job application after job application has been rejected because no one wants to take a chance that he will reoffend. But Mike Smith perseveres, in part, he says, because of the self-confidence and communication skills he developed when he was a member of Shakespeare Behind Bars.

'Here I am, out for three years,' he tells me, 'and to this day, if you asked me about anything out there at Luckett, I would say, "Shakespeare". I think you could contribute 70 to 80 percent of my success to it. That program was just such a benefit to all of us. When you talk about Sam and DeMond and some of those guys, they're role models out there. Sam is just a great guy. Stays out of trouble; does what he's supposed to. I worked with him as a programmer. DeMond, on the other hand, I kind of got to see his transition, because when he first got into the Shakespeare program he was kind of a rough guy. If you could've seen him over three, four, five years, he's just done an about-face. And you have to say to yourself, "Would DeMond have been taking college classes and studying religion if he hadn't met Shakespeare, if he hadn't met Curt?" DeMond didn't seem like he was heading that way. It's the Shakespeare program that changed him. It's the Shakespeare program that changed all of us.'

'What I did was shameful,' Mike says. 'I think of my potential and what I could be doing now. I'm busting my butt to get ahead, but it's just so hard. My dad tells me constantly that he knew when it happened the rest of my life was going to be difficult to get people to give me a chance. And that's the toughest part. Right now, things are good. I mean, overall, my worst day out here is better than my best day in there. And there's no way I would ever go back. I'm just so much stronger. I've had so much one-on-one, so much group work. There are so many techniques I've learned that I mean there's no way something like that could happen again.'

Mike can't believe it happened to begin with. 'I mean, when I pulled a knife on my girlfriend and her mother and threatened them, I knew what I did was wrong. Eight years and ten months is punishment. It didn't take me that long to figure out that I screwed up; I knew right then and there I made a big mistake. But you can't dwell on it. I don't want to sound as though I lack any empathy or sympathy for the victims, but it's something you really have to say, "I know what happened. I'm responsible for it." And you just have to know what you've done and the magnitude of it, but you've also got to say, "I'm passed that. I've dealt with it. I hope they have." And you can only hope that they have. But, I mean, I've got to move on. Because that would be really unhealthy just to dwell on that incident. It's tough. It takes a long time. Sooner or later you have say, "Hey, I'm a decent guy. I just made a mistake."'

The talk of decent men who just made mistakes puts Mike in mind of his best friend at Luckett, Sammie Byron.

'It's not right that I've been out for three years and Sam's still inside and going through the same routine,' Mike says. 'And his parole was recently denied. I just can't believe that after 20 years they thought he needed that much more time. It blows my mind. I think I could pick who deserves parole out there better than the board because when you're out there you see who's genuine and who's not. There's 2,000 guys out there. You could talk to every one of them, and every one knows Sammie Byron. He's got weightlifting titles; he's head of data entry. KCI is a big industry for Corrections and if you took Sammie out of there they'd probably have to shut data entry down. I don't even think their own supervisor could run that place as efficiently as Sam does. He's umpire for softball games, and people respect Sam because he's a towering figure. Sam's a role model. That's why when Sammie was denied parole, the guys were like, "If they didn't let Sammie go, what's going to happen to me?"'

Any concerns that Shakespeare graduates like Sammie might reoffend once they're released are unfounded, Mike argues. 'With people who's committed crimes like me or Sammie or whatever, you should worry more about the guy over there in the next restaurant booth rather than me because I don't know what's going on in his mind. I know what I've been through, and I know what I never want to go through again. I mean there is nothing that's gonna upset me to the point where I would ever commit a crime. Somebody could come up and spit in my face and, you know, I don't want any trouble. Really. It's not an option. Plain and simple. There's no reason for anybody to fear someone being released back into society unless they're the small percentage that says, "Hey, I played dominoes and cards, and I didn't go to the sex offenders treatment program; I didn't want to." Those are the guys you need to worry about. But when it comes to guys like Sammie Byron and DeMond Bush and Jerry Guenthner and Ron

Brown, I really think if you gave them a chance that they'd make it.'

After having spent so much time with Sammie and DeMond and Big G and Ron, I find myself agreeing with Mike that the men deserve 'a chance'. But it's not up to us. It's up to the parole board. It's up to the judge. And they don't see it our way.

In November 2004, DeMond Bush meets with the parole board. He is denied. In September 2005, Ron Brown requests resentencing. He is denied. In February 2006, Big G goes up for parole. He is denied. Big G receives a five-year deferment. DeMond is given a 10-year deferment. Ron is told that he will have to wait another 13 years before he sees the parole board for the first time. By that point, the trio will have spent a total of 72 years behind bars.

When I visit the men again, spirits are low. A prison employee has accused Sammie of tampering with the computer system. DeMond is pulled in for questioning. Though Sammie is eventually proved innocent of all charges, he and DeMond are shipped to a prison six hours away. Lonely without his friends, Ron puts in for a transfer to another prison on the opposite side of the state. Those Shakespeare Behind Bars members who remain at Luckett are distraught. Their family has been split up; they've been separated from their brothers. In light of the recent events, the Shakespeare group decides to forego their plan to produce *Timon of Athens* in favor of something more upbeat. They've earned the right to put on a comedy, they say. Their choice? *The Comedy of Errors*.

Shakespeare in Solitary: 'To Revenge or to Forgive?': *Hamlet* and *Othello* at the Wabash Valley Correctional Facility

'Be ready for anything,' Laura Bates warns me under her breath as she maneuvers two milk crates into place in the narrow hallway of the Secured Housing Unit at Wabash Valley Correctional Facility (WVCF). A super-maximum security prison in Indiana, WVCF was featured on the National Geographic channel as one of 'America's Hardest Prisons' in a documentary which characterized the institution as a place full of 'gang violence, attacks on staff, drug dealing and self-mutilation' and the WVCF inmates as 'the toughest and meanest prisoners in the US.' The film focused, in particular, on the Secured Housing Unit, or the SHU as it's called, in which '300 inmates are kept isolated for 23 hours a day to protect the rest of the prison inmates from their violent outbursts, sometimes brought on by mental illness' ('America's Hardest Prisons'). Those inmates who are sentenced to the SHU are enclosed in small, windowless cells with thick steel doors. Once a day for 30 minutes, they are escorted, individually, to the end of the hallway, which opens into an outdoor concrete cage. The men are able to look up the 40 feet of concrete walls and see the sky, but there are no trees, no birds, no grass. Some of them haven't seen any signs of nature in a decade.

'What is it like, living like that?' I ask one inmate, who spent three-and-a-half years in the SHU before being released into the general population.

'Nothing,' he replies politely. I offer an understanding smile.

'That's okay if you don't want to talk to me about it,' I tell him.

'No, ma'am,' he says, shaking his head. 'You ask me what it's like? I'm answering you. It's like nothing. You do nothing, you feel nothing, you see nothing, you are nothing.'

As if on cue, Laura and I look at each other. 'Nothing will come of nothing,' she says. I nod. Lear's words never seemed more appropriate.

No one wants to be sent to solitary, but Laura Bates, an English professor at Indiana State University, has been doing time in the SHU for years. The WVCF administrative staff couldn't be more accommodating and supportive of her program, 'Shakespeare in the SHU,' in which the men in segregation choose a Shakespeare play and rewrite it scene by scene, adapting the language into contemporary prose and the themes into life lessons for the convicted and incarcerated. The adaptation is then performed by Shakespeare Locked Down, Bates's prison drama group, which is comprised of general population inmates, and videotaped so that the SHU participants can see their work come to life. This year the play is *Hamlet*, and the inmates have chosen not only to update the language but, more importantly, to change the ending.

'Have a seat,' Laura tells me, pointing to the milk crate. We sit with our backs to the control room and face the end of the hallway. Lining either side of the hallway are temporary holding cells. The cells on the right have large letters painted on them; the cells on the left have numbers. By the time Laura and I arrive, the prison guards have already ushered the inmates down the hall and into the cells. As Laura walks down the hallway, each man calls out to her, his face pressed up against the only opening in the cell: the cuff-port, a waist-level, 10-inch slot that guards use for passing medicine and food to inmates and for cuffing their hands before transporting them to other areas of the prison. Six members this week, Laura notes with satisfaction. That's a good turnout. She's pleased. Sometimes the men in the Shakespeare program have a tendency toward irregular attendance. I wonder what they could possibly be doing instead.

'Mmm, mmm, mmm,' the voice in Cell 5 whispers to me through the tiny port in his cell. 'I've missed a couple of sessions these last weeks, but I'm here now. And damn, I picked a *good* day to come back to Shakespeare!'

The slot in the door is so small that I can't even see all of his face; I can only see his eyes looking out at me. It's like talking to someone who's in a mailbox. Actually, to be more precise, it's like talking to someone who *is* a mailbox. I feel like I'm in an absurdist drama, like someone has cast us all in a Beckett play, against our will.

'What's your name?' Cell 5 persists, flirting with me. 'You've got a vivaciousness about you.'

'Is that what they're calling it these days?' I quip.

Cell 5 laughs. 'You're feisty, too. I like that.'

I good-naturedly shake my head and roll my eyes to deflect his attention, but as unexpected as my exchange with Cell 5 might be, there's something comforting about the notion that years and years of solitary confinement can't erase every instinct in a human being. These men still have senses of humor, not to mention other interests.

Right now, they're interested in Shakespeare. At least, most of them are. To one new member, Shakespeare is like a foreign language. As the veterans set to work reading their adaptations of the duel scene to each other, the new guy in Cell 6 yells out in frustration, 'Yo, I got a question. Am I going to get a certificate for this or what? I only came 'cause they told me I could get a certificate.'

Laura assures him that he'll receive a certificate after he completes an entire season of Shakespeare, not just one session. 'Hey, man,' Cell 6 responds, 'I ain't never read a Shakespeare play in my life.' And Cell 6 doesn't sound especially eager to start now.

From across the hallway, Cell D calls out words of encouragement. 'When I first had Shakespeare given to me, I put the book on my floor and didn't pick it up again for maybe a year. It was hard at first to comprehend what the dude was saying. At first I didn't like that crap.'

Cell 4 agrees. He didn't like Shakespeare initially either, but then he realized the Bard's timelessness. 'If you're up on intellect and game and if you come from the ghetto, there's a lot of that in these plays,' Cell 4 shouts down the hallway to Cell 6. 'Shakespeare is real shit, man.'

Although most of the men can't see each other – they can see Laura and me sitting in the hallway, but they can't see each other – that doesn't keep them from communicating. 'You're going to have to be really loud,' Laura instructs Cell 4 as he begins to read his *Hamlet* adaptation, handwritten on notebook paper. 'We've got a big group today, and there are people four doors down from you.' The man raises his voice and continues reading, as if communicating with unseen people by shouting into a hallway is the most normal activity on earth.

As the men take turns reading their work, Laura hands me a copy of the SHU *Hamlet* adaptation in progress, and I leaf through the text. Some of the changes to Shakespeare's play are remarkable. In response to Hamlet's plan to catch the king's conscience by observing Claudius's reaction to *The Mousetrap*, for instance, Horatio accuses Hamlet of being 'an obvious Priam sympathizer' and argues that it is not ethical to gauge a person's innocent or guilt based upon his demeanor in public. 'If you were on trial, you should hope your conviction resulted from more than your reaction in court,' Horatio chides Hamlet. 'Don't you see your own prejudice? I'm not arguing that Claudius is innocent, I'm just trying to be an unbiased judge because justice is impossible otherwise.'

Today, however, the SHU Shakespeareans must decide how to end their play. 'We spoke about the *Hamlet* ending this week in our cages,' Cell D informs Laura. 'We talked about how to change it and make it better.' Though they disagree on what happens during the Hamlet–Laertes duel, they all agree that Hamlet should not kill anyone. This is the scene in which Laertes must forgive Hamlet, and Hamlet must forgive Claudius. When faced with the question: 'To revenge or not to revenge?', Hamlet must choose the latter. Choosing vengeance could only land him in one of two places – dead, or in solitary.

From Cell E, a deep, rich, bass voice explains why Shakespeare's ending is unacceptable. 'At the end of Shakespeare's play, almost everyone is dead. Shakespeare's message is that if you live by the sword, you gonna die by the sword. But Shakespeare doesn't offer an alternative to the violence. Is this the message we're trying to send society, particularly the youth? No. We want people to think about the consequences of their decisions. So in our play, one of the characters has to stop forward and make a speech. Hamlet should make the speech. He needs to say to Laertes, "I don't want to become what my father was. I don't want to become what your father was. We've got to break this cycle, man, the two of us, right here and right now." Hamlet has to explain why he decides not to take revenge.'

After the session ends, the guards return to the hallway and begin removing the first inmate from his cell and walking him to his cage. The others wait patiently for their turns; it's standard procedure to move one inmate at a time, and no one is in a hurry to leave Shakespeare and return to solitary. As Laura approaches Cell 6 to welcome him to the group, I stand in the middle of the hallway, not knowing what to do. 'Hey, come here,' Cell E orders me. Obediently, I walk to his cell. 'You a Shakespeare professor?' he asks me.

'Yes,' I reply.

'You think you might start a program like this some day?' he continues.

'Maybe,' I say.

'Well,' he tells me, 'just remember, if you have a Shakespeare program for inmates, you gotta let it belong to the inmates as well as yourself. You gotta let it be a dialogue. They talk and then you respond. It's important that they're allowed to voice their own interpretations, and it's important that you give feedback and respond to them. Because I can tell you, I've been locked up in solitary confinement for years now, and there's nothing worse. People are social beings. They need to be able to participate in conversations. There's nothing worse than not being spoken to. It's worse than not being able to talk. Remember that, now.'

'I'll remember,' I say.

As if it would be possible to forget anything about my visit to solitary, the eyes peering through the slots, the voices calling out from within the cells. While I stand outside of Cell E, three armed guards approach Cell 6. Cell 6 sticks his hands through the port, and the guards cuff his wrists and open the door. When the man walks out, I feel something like shock to realize that the two eyes behind the steel door belong to a real, live human being. At first I can't recognize him outside of his cell, and I stare him up and down, trying to adjust my perception. Gradually I persuade myself that he's not just a pair of eyes; he has a whole face, a whole body; he is a whole person. The guards shackle his legs, attach a metal leash to his belly chain and pull on it, leading him back to his solitary cage. As the man from Cell 6 slowly shuffles down the hallway, his face expressionless, his head bowed and eyes lowered, I return to the man in Cell E. 'I'll remember what you said,' I tell him again. And I think to myself, Ay, poor ghost. While memory holds a seat in this distracted globe. I have sworn't.

That afternoon Laura meets with Shakespeare Locked Down, her group of general population inmates. In accord with the SHU writers' wishes, the SLD actors agree that at the end of *Hamlet*, the title character will refuse to duel Laertes and refuse to kill Claudius. But the SLD group is even more excited about the second half of their show: they have decided to follow the *Hamlet* adaptation with an abbreviated version of *Othello* in Shakespeare's original verse. The double bill is entitled *To Revenge or Not to Revenge*.

As I arrive to the final dress rehearsal, one of the men is reciting their show's closing monologue: Shylock's 'Hath Not a Jew Eyes' speech from *The Merchant of Venice*. Although we've only just met, the inmate hands me a copy of the speech printed on a single piece of paper. 'Will you give me my lines in case I messed up?'

'Of course,' I assure him. And he begins.

> If it will feed nothing else,
> It will feed my revenge. He hath disgrac'd me,
> Hind'red me half a million, laugh'd at my losses,
> Mock'd at my gains, scorned my nation, thwarted my
> Bargains, cooled my friends, heated mine enemies,
> And what's the reason? I am a Prisoner.

Later, the inmate tells me that his reason for replacing the word 'Jew' with 'Prisoner' was to avoid saying anything that might be misinterpreted as disrespectful or intolerant. Though gang activity and ethnic slurs are prevalent in many prisons, WVCF has a particular history of 'racial conflict,' as the Human Rights Watch put it in their

1997 study at WVCF ('Cold Storage'). Nevertheless, whatever the inmate's motivation for inserting the word 'Prisoner', Shylock's speech takes on a whole new meaning when spoken by an inmate to the world at large, as though 'Prisoner' is its own demographic category, the lowest rung on the ladder. The actor continues.

> Hath not a Prisoner eyes? Hath not a Prisoner hands,
> Organs, dimensions, senses, affections, passions?
> Fed with the same food, hurt with the same weapons,
> Subject to the same diseases, healed by the same means,
> Warmed and cooled by the same winter and summer
> As Society is? – If you prick us do we not bleed?
> If you tickle us do we not laugh? If you poison us
> Do we not die? And if you wrong us shall we not
>   revenge?
> If we are like you in the rest, we will
> Resemble you in that. If a Prisoner wrong Society,
> What is his sufferance? Revenge! If Society wrong a
>   Prisoner,
> What should his sufferance be by Society's own
>   example?
> Why, revenge!

The actor pauses, as if he's forgotten the text.

'The villainy you teach me . . .' I prompt, wincing at the irony of the situation.

'I know,' he says.

'The villainy you teach me I will *not* execute!' he exclaims, determinedly pounding his fist into his hand to accentuate his addition to Shakespeare's text. 'And it shall go *hard,*' he admits, staring directly at me with a look so honest it moves me to tears. 'But I will better the instruction.'

As the actor leaves the stage and steps into the audience, his peers applaud. 'I like it that you added the word "not" man,' they say.

'Yeah,' the inmate responds. 'That's the whole point, that society is going to keep mistreating and seeking revenge. But we've made a commitment to be different from now on.'

At that moment, the actor playing Othello arrives to rehearsal. One of the most talented members of the SLD group, Greg Miller [not his real name] has single-handedly edited the *Othello* text, recruited most of the actors from amongst his friends, and blocked many of the key scenes. Additionally, Greg, a self-taught musician, has promised to open and close the show with two of his original songs, which he describes to me as half Othello's words, half his own. But during dress rehearsal, Greg is reluctant to take the stage. 'I'll sing the songs tomorrow,' he tells Laura. 'Let's just go ahead with the play for now.'

'He's shy, isn't he?' I ask an inmate sitting next to me.

'Yeah, but he's been locked up since he was a teenager,' the inmate replies with a voice full of respect for Greg. 'He's spent half his life in prison, and he's only 28.'

Finally, reluctantly, Greg walks to the stage and picks up his guitar. Greg is a Blues man, and when he sings, each word sounds like a thousand tears. 'Okay, this is going to be the song that opens the show,' he tells everyone. He pounds out the chords on his guitar like he's beating out a dirty rug, and then he opens his mouth and howls into the microphone.

> To revenge or to forgive?
> Decide what choice is right.
> All acts have consequences.
> What is owed must be paid.

In the chorus Greg plays off of Othello's language, promising his audience,

> We will rise; we will do what is right.
> We will try to make it up to you.

It is our cause.
It is our cause.
It is our cause.
A second chance.

As with the Shylock speech, the SLD production of *Othello* has all of the racial and ethnic references edited out of the text. 'It's not a play about race,' Greg, a white man, tells me. 'It's a play about class. Othello is a soldier, and that's why Desdemona's father doesn't like him.' Greg's response gives me pause. It's not simply that this explanation doesn't align with Shakespeare's play – Othello isn't just a soldier; he's the general of the Venetian army, for God's sake – it's more that there's something in Greg's voice that suggests even he doesn't buy his explanation. Why, I wonder, is it so important to Greg to play this role, because clearly he identifies with Shakespeare's Moor. If *Othello* isn't a play about racial conflict, then what is it about? 'It's just important to Greg, that's all,' one of his friends tells me.

The same air of mystery hangs over the rehearsal of the scene in which Othello murders Desdemona. The inmates have practiced this scene in their dorms, with Greg dictating most of the blocking. In lieu of an actual bed, Desdemona sleeps on a table. Remarkably, at the end of the play, after the other actors have left the stage, Desdemona *remains* on the table, dead, as Greg reaches for his guitar, walks to the microphone, and performs one last song. Laura suggests that Desdemona leave the stage with everyone else, or that they at least cover her over with a blanket. The men are hesitant. They look around at each other but ignore Laura's suggestion. For some unspoken reason, it's very important to them to keep Desdemona visible. The following day, during the actual performance, they pull the blanket over Desdemona's legs, as if to respect Laura's instructions, but they leave Desdemona's face and upper body visible to the audience, crossing her arms as they exit the stage. The SLD actors' decision to keep the victim onstage sets their performance apart from most television shows and films about prison, which have a tendency to focus on the inmates' stories rather than taking into account the victims' stories. In the SLD production of *Othello*, the men leave the victim on the table, literally, as if to say, 'We haven't forgotten what we've done. We haven't forgotten that we've hurt people.' It is, to say the least, a very compelling tableau.

As the dead Desdemona lies there, center stage, Greg begins his song:

> I'm angry at you for
> Leaving me here all alone
> After fighting this war.
> Now that it's over,
> I want to come home.
>
> Is there a place for me,
> Or have you replaced my love?
> We'll make a family,
> New memories.
> Oh, I want to come home.
>
> I don't want to be alone
> After fighting this war.
> I don't want to be alone
> Without your love.

After the show, I ask Greg what his song means. 'I'm singing to my sister,' he explains. 'That part about wanting to be a family and make new memories, that's for her. I wanted to sing it to her today, but she didn't come the performance. I'll sing it to her eventually, though.'

It's not until the following day, and after a certain amount of research, that I find out Greg has a 60-year sentence for a double homicide. You wouldn't know it from looking at him. Clean cut, handsome, polite, talented, Greg seems like he should be in a college honor society rather than a maximum-security prison. There's nothing about the Greg I met to indicate that he is the same young man who, when he was only 14 years old, on a quiet February evening, in a small town in rural Indiana, picked up a gun, walked into his sleeping parents' bedroom, and shot them in the head. When I learn about Greg's story, including his subsequent estrangement from his older sister, I replay the second stanza of his song in my mind.

> It's a tragedy,
> You and me,
> The life I've taken from you.
> I forced myself to do
> What I didn't want to.
> Let it get to me.
>
> Now you're gone
> Put out the light
> In darkness I am gone.
> It'll never burn again,
> Can't be relit.
> I don't want to be alone.
>
> I don't want to be alone
> After fighting this war.
> I don't want to be alone
> Without your love.

In my car, as I drive home from Indiana, I can't get Greg's song out of my mind. I think about Greg's parents. I think about his sister. I think about Greg himself, the young man with the voice that sounds like crying. And all the while, in the back of my head, is the image of Desdemona, lying on the table, dead.

Epilogue

One specific thing that's really hard for me to deal with is that many of the guys are in here for crimes against women and children. I'm like, 'Man, you did this to what? Why did you do that? How could you do that?' And then I come to understand: they didn't just wake up one day and decide that they was gonna rape a woman or hurt a kid. They went through it in their childhood and they have problems that they have to deal with. You can either push them aside, or you can accept them if they have empathy for their victim and take responsibility for what they did and try to develop a plan of action. 'Why did you do that? What triggered that kind of problem in your life that would make you act out like that?' And hope it all works out somehow.

Jerry 'Big G' Guenthner

Throughout my series of interviews with the Shakespeare Behind Bars participants, I notice that most of them have taken responsibility for their crimes. While they are not necessarily eager to talk about their pasts and while they certainly hope that they will not be associated with their crimes for the rest of their lives, they do not evade my questions. Many of them announce their crimes just minutes into their interviews, without any instigation from me. 'I'm in here for killing a police officer,' Big G tells me. 'I've got a murder charge, ma'am,' says Vaughn, before I can even ask. 'I committed sex crimes against children,' says Leonard. 'And that's a horrible thing.' Yes it is, I think to myself.

Leonard is well acquainted with the feeling of being despised for his crimes. Leonard sexually molested seven little girls. Even in prison, where murderers and drug dealers might have a certain amount of prestige, pedophiles are considered the scum of the earth. Leonard comments on 'the prejudices and stereotypes and fear and the outright hatred that is directed toward pedophiles. It just crushes me that my humanity is cloaked by that word "pedophile", that I am defined by these acts.'

'I received a 50-year sentence,' Leonard tells me. 'I could have received a 20-year sentence, but I named my victims so that they wouldn't have to go to trial. I didn't want them to put the kids on the stand and make them relive it, so I had no choice. Fifty years. And if I get paroled, I'll go out, I'll get a job, and I'll live well, and I'll live with honor, and I will not harm anyone, much less a child, again. But that's if. Fifty years. I could die in prison. And so I just say, "This is my life. I'm just going to live here in this moment." The quality of my life externally is pretty abysmal, but internally it's very powerful and very beautiful to me. And I try to focus there. I'm a Shakespearean actor. And I can't leave the theatre.'

Shakespeare Behind Bars, Hank Rogerson's 2005 documentary film about the group at Luckett, does not spend much time considering the victims' lives and deaths; instead the film strives to remind audiences of the very real and important fact that social deviants and criminals are often themselves victims of brutal violence, both during their childhoods, before they commit their crimes, and during adulthood, as they continue to be subjected to abuse and mistreatment in prison. Out of the four men who reveal their pasts in the *Shakespeare Behind Bars* film, three of them confess to crimes against women or little girls. In a documentary that is structured around the themes of forgiveness and redemption, the film delivers the audience the ultimate challenge by putting the message of forgiveness into the mouth of an inmate that may be the most difficult to forgive, a convicted pedophile. That inmate is Leonard Ford. In the film, Leonard explains that during rehearsals of *The Tempest* he's been thinking about two lines in particular, the conclusion of Prospero's epilogue 'As you from crimes would pardoned be | Let your indulgence set us free,' and he offers his own application of Shakespeare's message to his present situation: 'What Shakespeare calls "indulgence", and what has been my single greatest desire since October 1994, is to be redeemed. All of us, in some way, need to be redeemed. I would like to redeem my life so that I'm not remembered for the very worst thing that I've done.' Leonard concludes, as if anticipating his audience's reluctance to forgive him, 'The people who need mercy are the ones that deserve it the least.'

For the woman who sat next to me when the film premiered at the Sundance Film Festival, this challenge was too much. She and her friend had arrived at the cinema at 8.30 that morning to stand in line for hours in order to get a ticket to the sold-out documentary. As a lover of Shakespeare and someone interested in prison reform, she was inclined to like the film. But on their way out of the cinema, I overheard her say to her friend, 'I don't care how sorry he is. I don't care how good of an actor he is. I don't care how much we both love Shakespeare. I don't forgive someone who molests little girls.' Her friend quietly nodded in agreement, crumpled up her program and threw it in the trash.

When I recount this story to one of my colleagues on the phone that evening, he responds, 'Well, if they hadn't done something wrong, then it wouldn't be called forgiveness. It would just be an exercise in self-congratulation.' The act of forgiveness, by definition, requires someone to have committed an offense.

During the process of researching this book, there have been moments of supreme joy, of downright glee. Every one of those moments has happened during my time in prison. Those moments have come not only while watching a rehearsal or performance but also when hanging out with the inmates in the Visitor's Room, talking about everything from Dave Chappelle's television show to Audrey Hepburn to the Atkins Diet. But in every case when I found myself saying in my head, 'This is fun!' there was always an incident to bring me back down to earth and remind me that I wasn't in a theatre; I was in prison. A rape on the yard. An officer covered in blood and dirt from having broken up a fight between inmates. A reminder of the unnamed, voiceless victims and survivors, the ones who don't get books written about them.

One of the most important reminders, for me, came in September 2005 when Ron Brown asked me to attend his resentencing hearing.

That day, I arrived at the county courthouse and headed to the clerk's office so I could find out which room the hearing was in. There were about six clerks, but they were all busy playing with someone's little boy who was there for a visit. As I waited at the window, a woman came in and stood to my side. A clerk came forward, and the woman stepped up to the window. 'I'm here for the resentencing hearing for Ronald Anthony Brown,' she said. For a split second, I almost shouted out, 'Oh, I'm here for that, too!' For a split second, I assumed that she was a friend of Ron's, there to support him. For a split second, I turned to her, smiling. She paid no attention to me. And just as quickly as I had made my mistake, I realized that I was looking in the face of the victim's family member. She said Ron's full name – 'Ronald Anthony Brown' – as though pronouncing the entire name would distance herself from him. I said nothing. A younger woman came in the room, presumably her daughter, a beautiful woman, stylishly dressed and carefully groomed, in her mid-30s. My age. The clerk pointed the way to the judge's chambers, and they left, never looking at me. I doubt if they even saw me, or the clerk, or anyone they had encountered all day long, for that matter. They seemed to be saving their energy for the ordeal at hand. I imagined that, as far as these women were concerned, they were going into battle. Ironically, the only way to find the battlefield was to name the enemy – 'Ronald Anthony Brown.' They should've been able to name their beloved instead, the one they had lost, the one that Ronald Anthony Brown had taken away from them. Instead, there they were, forever separated from their beloved and forever linked to a convict. And so, if the name of the enemy had to be said, let it be said entirely. 'Ronald Anthony Brown.' Say it slowly and precisely so that there would be no more mistakes, no more accidents, no more losses. 'Ronald Anthony Brown.' Say it with such quiet rage that anyone who hears you will know what you're really saying: 'I'm here for the resentencing of Ronald Anthony Brown. That monster who murdered my husband.'

Of course, at that point, I didn't know what the woman's relationship was to the victim. Mother, sister, wife – I didn't know. I only knew what her relationship was to Ron. It was 30 minutes before the hearing. I had planned to go straight to the judge's chambers, but instead I went outside for some air. There I was, an ardent feminist, someone who had felt endangered and victimized in the past, and I was going to sit by the side of the enemy, by the side of the man who hurt these women. I thought about leaving. Instead, I decided to go down the end of the walkway to wait for Curt to arrive.

When I reached the sidewalk, there was the woman again, smoking a cigarette. She was pale and gaunt and wrinkled. I looked at her without saying anything. She looked at me without seeing anyone. I imagined that in her head, she was already in the hearing. In her head, she was back at the trial. In her head, she was at the funeral. In her head, it was the morning – *that* morning – and she was saying goodbye to her beloved, not knowing that it would be the last time she would see him alive. She put out the cigarette and marched back inside the courthouse.

Curt arrived, with his costume designer Michelle Bombe, and his wife Marcia by his side, and we headed into the judge's chambers. Ron was outside in the hallway, wearing an orange jumpsuit. His legs were chained together, he had tight handcuffs on, and he was surrounded by two armed guards. He looked very small to me. Small and scared. As we entered the judge's chambers, we walked by him. Curt wished Ron luck. Ron said hello to each of us as we passed and thanked us for coming.

Inside the chambers, we weren't sure where to sit. There was one long conference table with chairs on either side. The judge's desk was at the front. A group of people, including the woman and her daughter, lined the far side of the room. I asked Michelle where we should sit. 'Along the opposite wall, I guess,' she said. Later she would tell me how sitting on the inmate's side made her feel the sort of disdain that a convict receives. Michelle wasn't able to look into the eyes of the victims' family. I did, but only in glances, my head bowed as a way to signal my respect. In addition to the woman and her daughter, there were an older man and woman, who looked to be in poor health. They were overweight, sloppily dressed, old before their time. The older woman was hard of hearing; her whispers sounded like shouting to me. 'Is that the guy he tried to pin it on?' she asked, pointing at Curt. 'No, that's not,' said the woman next to her. Well, who was he then? I watched the old woman as the realization sunk in: the new people in the room were not *against* Ron; the new people in the room were *for* Ron. In that case, the new people in the room must be enemies, too. While we waited, face to face, in silence, a pair of lawyers sat at the conference table, chatting about golf.

The judge entered the chambers, a kind, soft-spoken, gentle man. He immediately thanked us for standing, begged us to sit down, and then adjusted the thermostat on the wall to make sure that the room temperature was comfortable for us. Then Ron entered the room, flanked by the guards and followed by his lawyer. Several new letters written by the victim's family were presented to Ron, and the judge gave him time to read them. Ron's lawyer asked if Ron could downgrade to a pair of less restrictive handcuffs so that he would be able to turn the pages of the letters. Before the judge answered, one guard spoke up. 'I wouldn't advise that, your honor. The convict can only have another pair of handcuffs with the court's permission, and I would advise against that.' The judge respected the guard's decision. 'I'm okay,' Ron said, his head bowed.

After Ron read the letters, his lawyer proceeded. The lawyer said very little, and really only served as the person to introduce Ron.

Then Ron spoke. He had been preparing for this moment for years, I knew. He acknowledged his guilt. He apologized. He looked directly at the victim's family, and apologized again and again and again. His apology lasted for more than 15 minutes. No one interrupted him. No one said anything. The woman shed a few tears. The daughter wept openly, looking straight at Ron. Out of all the people, Ron spoke directly to her, tears streaming down his own face. Ron wanted to make it clear that it was not a racially-motivated crime, as some of the letters written by the victim's family had claimed. He wanted to make it clear that he loved his 14-year-old daughter, even though some of the letters had suggested he didn't. He wanted to let the people know that he had changed. But most of all, he wanted to say that he was sorry.

When he finished, the opposing lawyers spoke. 'I am sure that Mr Brown is sorry,' the lead attorney said, and, surprisingly, the attorney brought up Shakespeare. 'Mr Brown has taken advantage of several programs in prison, including a drama program. Mr Brown has become a persuasive actor. But the fact of the matter is that he committed a heinous crime. He stole a car, kidnapped Mr _____, and shot him. Mr Brown says that he wishes he could have changed the situation. He could have. He could have sought medical attention for Mr _____. Instead, he shoved his body in the back seat, turned up the radio so that he couldn't hear Mr _____ cry for help, and drove across state lines. Mr Brown says that he misses his daughter. Mr _____'s parents miss their son. Mr _____'s friends miss their friend. Mr _____'s fiancée misses her boyfriend.'

I looked at the beautiful young woman, sitting across from me. So she wasn't the victim's daughter. She was his fiancée. I looked at her left hand, hoping to find a wedding band, hoping that she had married someone else, found love, found happiness, found something. There was no ring. As the lawyer spoke, she sat staring directly at Ron, with sadness but also with a certain kind of softness in her eyes. He returned her gaze. It was almost as though *they* had become the couple. In their looking was something like love.

The lawyer continued, 'Mr Brown was tried by a jury of his peers, found guilty, and given a just sentence. Now he has to complete that sentence.'

Ultimately, the judge agreed. The very kind judge explained to Ron that although he believed Ron was sorry, although Ron's prison record was 'exemplary' and he was a 'model prisoner and in some ways an inspiration,' the judge had come to believe that the justice system usually works, and in this case, Ron had been tried by a jury of his peers and given a fair sentence. As the judge ruled that Ron would have to serve his entire sentence, the victim's family members smacked their hands together in celebration. The beautiful woman did not react at all. She just sat there, staring at Ron with her gentle gaze.

Ron was immediately whisked out of the room. The judge left. As Curt, Marcia, Michelle, and I headed toward the elevator, Ron's lawyer stopped us to thank us for attending the hearing. 'Ron's changed just in the year I've been representing him,' he told us. 'I'm sorry that I couldn't get his sentence reduced.'

'That's not what it was about,' Curt replied as he wheeled his wife into the elevator, 'It was about Ron having a chance to apologize.' When I spoke with him months later, however, Ron acknowledged that the judge's decision sent him into a period of deep depression, a period during which he even contemplated suicide. It *was* about Ron having a chance to apologize for taking someone's life, but it was also about Ron hoping for a second chance to live his own, this time on the other side of the razor-wire.

Today, after having transferred back to Luther Luckett Correctional Complex, Ron Brown has rejoined Shakespeare Behind Bars just in time to cast himself as Vincentio in *Measure for Measure*. At Northeast, Lavell Webb has been preparing to reprise the role of Mark Antony in *Julius Caesar, Act V*. At Wabash Valley, Greg Miller has been practicing his *Othello* songs in preparation for the time when he can sing them to his sister. These men know only too well that Shakespeare is not a cure-all for the challenges they face. In life, and especially in prison life, there is always the possibility of disappointment and despair, and even recidivism. Sometimes, the people who matter most don't forgive you, sometimes you don't get a second chance, and Shakespeare can't change that. Shakespeare can't change what your father did to you when you were a boy. Shakespeare can't bring your victim back to life. Shakespeare can't make your sister visit you. Shakespeare can't keep you safe behind bars. Shakespeare can't make the parole board grant your release. But Shakespeare can give you someone to talk to, characters who are like old friends, and who are able to express exactly what you've been feeling for years but haven't been able to articulate yourself; others who are all too familiarly flawed, and whose behavior may challenge you to re-examine your own life, or maybe just rejoice in the knowledge that every person makes mistakes and bad choices at some point; others who make you laugh, even in prison, even when there is nothing worth laughing about. Shakespeare programs can provide an intellectually stimulating environment and emotionally enriching community, a fraternity or sorority of friends who are there to offer their support, both during those times when you want to talk about Shakespeare and on those days when you haven't received a letter in weeks, or your lawyer doesn't show up for the fourth time in a row or you're tempted to start a fight with a bully on the yard. In a world where you're identified by a number, lined up and counted three times a day, or treated like an animal, chained and led by a leash, being a part of a Shakespeare group can help you remember that you're a person. And for Ron, Lavell and Greg, that's exactly what Shakespeare programs do. For these inmates and others like them, Shakespeare is much more than a welcome distraction from the tedium, deprivation and dangers of prison life. Shakespeare is a creative, social and spiritual life force; a vital and necessary reminder that, no matter what, we are all human beings.

Bibliography

'America's Hardest Prisons,' National Geographic Channel, www.national geographic.co.uk/explore/prisons. Last accessed: 6 September 2006.

Berry, Cicely (1972). 'That Secret Voice,' in *Shakespeare Comes to Broadmoor*, edited by Murray Cox. London: Jessica Kingsley, pp. 189–200.

'Cold Storage: Super-maximum security confinement in Indiana,' (October 1997) Human Rights Watch. www.hrw.org/reports/1997/usind/

Haley, Alex (1987). *The Autobiography of Malcolm X*. New York: Ballantine.

Hauser, Thomas (1987). 'The Quotable Mr King and the Quotable Mr Hopkins,' *Seconds Out*. www.secondsout.com/USA/colhauser.cfm? ccs=208&cs=3925.

Herold, Niels. 'Shakespeare and the Performance of Rehabilitation,' Shakespeare Association of America 34th Annual Meeting. Philadelphia, PA: 15 April 2006.

Johnston, Chris (1998). 'Twisting Paradoxes,' in *Prison Theatre: Perspectives and Practices*, edited by James Thompson. London: Jessica Kingsley, pp. 127–42.

Melville, Joy. 'Ellen Terry: Greatest English actress of the 19th century,' http://womenshistory.about.com/library/prm/blellenterry2.htm. Last accessed: 13 July 2004.

Montgomery, Marianne. Email. 2 March 2005.

Nelly. 'Ride Wit' Me,' featuring City Spud. *Country Grammar*. Universal Records, 2000.

Rylance, Mark (1992). 'Hamlet and Romeo,' interview with Rob Ferris, in *Shakespeare Comes to Broadmoor*, edited by Murray Cox. London: Jessica Kingsley, pp. 27–42.

Saunders, Jessica (1992). 'Awakening the Voice Inside: Dramatherapy and theatre initiatives in prison,' in *Shakespeare Comes to Broadmoor*, edited by Murray Cox. London: Jessica Kingsley, pp. 221–7.

Shakespeare Behind Bars (2005) Directed by Hank Rogerson. Philomath Films.

Trounstine, Jean (2001). *Shakespeare Behind Bars: The power of drama in a women's prison*. New York: St Martins.

Wiltenburg, Mary (2002). 'Shakespeare Behind Bars: Acting with conviction.' Photos by Andy Nelson. *Christian Science Monitor* website. http://csmonitor.com/specials/shakespeare/

Personal Interviews

Bates, Laura: 21 August 2006.
Brown, Ron: 18 May 2004; 18 June 2004.
Bush, DeMond: 18 May 2004; 18 June 2004.
Byron, Sammie: 18 May 2004; 18 June 2004.
Cobb, Hal: 18 May 2004; 19 May 2004.
Chandler, Larry: 7 July 2004
Ford, Leonard: 19 May 2004.
Guenthner, Jerry: 18 May 2004.
Herriford, Marcel: 19 May 2004.
Hughes, Richard: 18 May 2004.
Norman, Tim: 19 January 2006.
Perachi, Paul: 11 April 2006.
Smith, Mike: 19 June 2004.
Tofteland, Curt: 17–20 May 2004.
Trounstine, Jean: 11 January 2006.
Vaughn, Floyd Gene: 19 May 2004.

Performances

Julius Caesar (17–20 May 2004). Directed by Curt Tofteland. Shakespeare Behind Bars: Luther Luckett. Correctional Complex. LaGrange, Kentucky.

Julius Caesar (3 September 2004). Directed by Curt Tofteland. Shakespeare Behind Bars: Kentucky Correctional Institute for Women. Pewee Valley, Kentucky. 3 September 2004.

Julius Caesar: Acts II and III (17–19 January 2006). Directed by Agnes Wilcox. Prison Performing Arts: Northeast Correctional Complex. Bowling Green, Missouri.

Othello Unplugged (7 July 2004). Directed by Curt Tofteland. Kentucky Shakespeare Festival: Luther Luckett Correctional Complex. LaGrange, Kentucky.

Rapshrew (6 June 1989). Directed by Jean Trounstine. Framingham Women's Prison. Framingham, Massachusetts.

To Revenge or Not to Revenge: Hamlet *and* Othello (21 August 2006). Directed by Laura Bates. Shakespeare in the SHU and Shakespeare Locked Down; Wabash Valley Correctional Facility. Carlisle, Indiana.

Recommended Sources on Shakespeare and Corrections

Baim, Clark (2004). '"If All the World's a Stage, Why Did I get the Worst Parts": Psychodrama with violent and sexually abusive men,' in *Theatre in Prison: Theory and Practice*, edited by Michael Balfour. Intellect: Bristol.

Bates, Laura Raidonis (2004). '"Here is Not a Creature but Myself": Shakespearean reception in solitary confinement,' *Shakespeare Yearbook 12*, pp. 122–30.

—— '"Shakespeare Sucketh" (2004–5). 'The Pros and Cons of Shakespeare in Correctional Education.' *Shakespeare and the Classroom* 12–13. Forthcoming.

—— 'The Uses of Shakespeare in Criminal Rehabilitation: Testing the limits of "universality,"' in *Shakespeare Matters: History, teaching, performance*, edited by Lloyd Davis. Newark: University of Delaware pp. 151–63.

Colbert, Stephen (20 April 2006). 'The Word: "Bard": Teaching kids Shakespeare will just make them more violent' [Farcical editorial on the Shakespeare in the courts' *Macbeth* Performance on 11 April 2006]. Episode 2051. *The Colbert Report:* Comedy Central.

'Exeunt Omnes' (23 February 2003). Episode 56. *Oz.* Screenplay by Tom Fontana. Directed by Alex Zakrzewski. HBO.

Fraden, Rena (2001). *Imagining Medea: Rhodessa Jones and theater for incarcerated women.* University of North Carolina: Chapel Hill.

Glass, Ira (9 August 2002). '*Hamlet*: Act Five.' *This American Life.* National Public Radio.

'Junkyard Dawgs' (16 February 2003). Episode 55. *Oz.* Screenplay by Tom Fontana and Chuck Schweizer. Directed by Ted Bogosian. HBO.

Kissinger, Meg (25 April 2005). 'Captivating Theater: Inmates at Racine Prison to stage production of *King Lear*,' in *Milwaukee Journal Sentinel.* www.jsonline.com/story/index.aspx?id=321129

Minkin, Melissa (September/October 2002). 'Shaking up Shakespeare' [article on the Los Angeles Shakespeare Festival's Will Power to Youth Program]. *Hope*, pp. 33–5.

Prison Performing Arts. www.prisonartsstl.org/projects.htm

Scott-Douglass, Amy (2007). 'All the World's a Stage,' in *Shakespeares After Shakespeare: An Encyclopedia of the Bard in Mass Media and Popular Culture*, general editor Richard Burt, contributing editor Amy Scott-Douglass. Westport, CT: Greenwood, 807.

— Review of *All the World's a Stage* at Luther Luckett Correctional Complex. *Early Modern Literary Studies* 11.1 (May 2005): 14.1–11.

— Review of *Julius Caesar* at Luther Luckett Correctional Complex. *Shakespeare Bulletin* 22.3 (Fall 2004): 66–70.

Taylor, Lori. 'Incarcerated Youth at Play: An ASP outreach program at the DYS facility in Dorchester,' *Actors' in Shakespeare Project Newsletter* 2.1 (Fall 2005), p. 2. www.actorsshakespeareproject.org/getinvolved/serpents.tongue.v2.1.pdf

Trounstine, Jean (Winter 1996–7). 'Sacred Spaces,' in *Journal of the Assembly for Expanded Perspectives on Language*, pp. 1–9.

Wall, Bruce. 'London Shakespeare Workshop Prison Project: Promoting confidence through the will to dream.' www.londonshakespeare.org.uk/prison/chairman01.htm

Wilgoren, Jodi. 'In One Prison, Murder Betrayal and High Prose,' in *New York Times*, 29 April 2005. www.nytimes.com/2005/04/29/national/29lear.html? ex=1272427200&en=1388e84b37d97549&ei=5090&partner=rssuserland&emc=rss

'Will Power to Youth,' Los Angeles Shakespeare Festival. www.shakespeare festivalla.org/wpy/index.htm

Zelon, Helen (October 2001). 'The Shakespeare Redemption: Inmates at a Kentucky prison grapple with the truths of human existence,' *American Theater*, pp. 32–5, 134–5.

Unpublished Work

Essays presented at the 'Prison Shakespeare' session led by Amy Scott-Douglass (amysd@denison.edu) at the Modern Language Association 121st Annual Convention, Washington DC, 29 December 2005:

Laura Raidonis Bates, lbates@isugw.indstate.edu, 'Shakespeare Saved My Life: Voices from a segregated housing unit'.

Meg Sempreora, sempreme@webster.edu, 'Performing "To Be": The Hamlet project of Prison Performing Arts'.

Curt Tofteland, tofter@aol.com, 'Shakespeare Behind Bars'.

Jean Trounstine, trounstinej@middlesex.mass.edu, 'Adapting Shakespeare: The power of drama in a women's prison'.

Essays presented as part of the 'Big-House Shakespeare' workshop led by Amy Scott-Douglass at the Shakespeare Association of America 34th Annual Meeting, Philadelphia, PA, 15 April 2006:

Melissa D. Aaron, maaron@csupomona.edu, 'Hath Not a Bitch Eyes?: All-female prison Shakespeare'.

Denise Albanese, dalbanes@gmu.edu, 'Making Shakespeare Matter: This American life and prison Shakespeare'.

Laura Raidonis Bates, lbates@isugw.indstate.edu, 'The Will to Kill: Macbeth's criminal nature'.

Niels Herold, herold@oakland.edu, 'Shakespeare and the Performance of Rehabilitation'.

Hank Rogerson, philomath@earthlink.net, '*Shakespeare Behind Bars:* A festival diary'.

Meg Sempreora, sempreme@webster.edu, 'Classics in Prison: Teaching in the round'.

Curt L. Tofteland, tofter@aol.com, 'We Few, We Happy Few, We Band of Brothers.'

Jean Trounstine, trounstinej@middlesex.mass.edu, 'Light in the Darkest Places.'

Agnes Wilcox, agnes@prisonartsstl.org, 'Belonging to the Rest of the World: Shakespeare's enduring lessons of hope.'

Index